# SECOND ACTS

for Solo and Small Firm Lawyers

jennifer j. rose
**editor**

AMERICAN BAR ASSOCIATION
**Senior Lawyers
Division**

Cover design by Amanda Fry/ABA Design

Printed in the United States of America.

23 22 21 20   5 4 3

**Library of Congress Cataloging-in-Publication Data**
Names: Rose, Jennifer (Jennifer J.), editor. | American Bar Association. Senior
    Lawyers Division, sponsoring body.
Title: Second acts for solo and small firm lawyers / edited by Jennifer J. Rose.
Description: Chicago : American Bar Association, 2019. | Includes index.
Identifiers: LCCN 2019006075 | ISBN 9781641054256 (print) | ISBN
    9781641054263 (epub)
Subjects: LCSH: Lawyers—Retirement—United States. | Retirement—United
    States—Planning.
Classification: LCC KF316.7 .S43 2019 | DDC 332.024/01402434—dc23
LC record available at https://lccn.loc.gov/2019006075

www.shopABA.org

# Contents

About the Editor    xi

About the Contributors    xiii

About This Book    xxiii

## Part I
## Deciding When It's Time to Leave    1

### Chapter 1
### Time to Retire    3
*Robin Page West*

### Chapter 2
### A Five-Year Plan for Active Retirement    11
*David Zachary Kaufman*

Introduction    11

Who Am I? Who Is "Me"?    12

What Did I Want from "Retirement"?    13

Implementation    13

    Stay or Go? Where to Live    13

    When to Retire Is Up to You    15

    When to Retire Depends on Your Financial Situation    15

    Your Life Experiences and Fitness Will Control What to Do
during Your Active Life    16

    Strangely Enough, I Still Love the Law    18

    Planning for the Future Career Is Critical    19

    Once You Have a Plan, Implement It    19

Lessons Learned (or Advice That's Worth Only What You Paid
for It)    20

**Chapter 3**
**You've Got Options, Lots and Lots and Lots of Options!    21**
*Jeffrey Allen*


**Chapter 4**
**A Nontraditional Law Firm Provides a Roadmap for Your Transition to Retirement    29**
*David J. Leffler*

The Empty Nester    30
Founder's Solution    31
World Traveler    32
Young Family    33
My Story    35
Your Turn    36


**Chapter 5**
**Scaling Back a Practice to Part-Time, Winding Down, and Changing Practice Specialties and Practice Styles    37**
*Robin Page West*


**Part II**
**When the Decision Is Not the Lawyer's Own    45**

**Chapter 6**
**How Cognitive Decline Affects Lawyers    47**
*Scott R. Mote*

Medical Implications    48
Types of Cognitive Impairment    50
    Dementia    50
    Alzheimer's Disease    51
    Delirium    51
    Mental Health Implications    51

The Effects of Cognitive Impairment on Lawyers and Clients   52
Bob, the Disorganized and Confused Lawyer   52
Gene, a Lawyer Who Misses Deadlines and Becomes Irritable When Questioned   53
Reporting   56
Create a Positive Environment   56

## Chapter 7
## Addressing Ethical Issues Facing the Aging Lawyer   59
*Ted A. Waggoner*

Pushing the Ethical Boundaries   59
Identifying and Resolving the Problems   61
Disciplinary Matters   63

## Chapter 8
## Strategies for Dealing with the Lawyer Who Refuses to Discuss Retirement   65
*Ted A. Waggoner*

Background Issues   66
Strategy 1: Plan Early   68
Strategy 2: The Partnership Agreement or Retirement Contract   69
Strategy 3: When Other Strategies Are Not Working   71
Tactics   73
Proving the Case   73
Countering the Defenses   74
Intervention   75
Protecting the Reputation   75
Increasing Problem for the Profession   75

# Part III
# Maintaining Ties with the Bar    77

## Chapter 9
## The Bar Is Our Home    79
*Marvin S.C. Dang*

Decades of ABA Involvement    80
Reasons to Stay Involved    83
It's Never Too Late to Get Involved    85
Some Final Thoughts    87

## Chapter 10
## Maintaining Your Status with the Bar    89
*Craig A. Stokes*

Continued Active Status    90
Retirement    91
"Inactive" Status    92
Conclusion    93

# Part IV
# Taking Work in Different Directions    95

## Chapter 11
## Morphing to Mediation: ADR as an Alternative    97
*David J. Abeshouse*

Additional Recommended Reading    105

## Chapter 12
## What Should I Do with What I Know?    107
*Lisa A. Runquist*

## Chapter 13
## Pro Bono Work after Retiring 113
*Joan M. Burda*

Emeritus Lawyer Programs 114

Legal Aid Programs 115

Hospice Organizations 116

Nonprofit Organizations 118

Court Pro Se Programs 118

Limited Scope Representation 119

Bar Association Opportunities 120

American Bar Association Programs 120

Malpractice Insurance 121

Varying Practice Areas 121

Wrapping Up 122

# Part V
# There's More to Life Than Practicing Law 123

## Chapter 14
## Finding Fulfillment by Serving on a Volunteer Board of Directors 125
*Jeffrey Allen*

## Chapter 15
## Confessions of a Recovering Divorce Lawyer 135
*Jimmy Verner*

## Chapter 16
## Teaching before and during Retirement   145
*Joan M. Burda*

You Won't Get Rich   145
Law School   146
Colleges, Universities, and Community Colleges   148
Adult Education Classes   150
Writing: Content, Freelance, Books, Articles   151

## Chapter 17
## RVing for Retiring Lawyers: Driving toward the Future   155
*Vicki Levy Eskin*

How Did I Start Out?   156
How Do I Do It?   157

## Chapter 18
## Retiring at My Own Speed   167
*Wendy Cole Lascher*

From Small to Big   168
Learning to Fly   169
    Stretching My Brain   170
    Transferring Skills   171

## Chapter 19
## From Courtroom to Cockpit   173
*Capt. David R. Hammer*

## Chapter 20
## Picture This: The Journey to My Second Act   181
*Victoria L. Herring*

# Part VI
# Strategizing Your Social Security Claim   191

## Chapter 21
## Social Security Benefits for You and Your Family   193
*Avram L. Sacks*

Introduction   193

Benefit Eligibility   195

The Difference between Early and Full Retirement   196

How a Benefit Is Calculated   198

Benefits Available to Dependents and Survivors   201

    Spouses   202

    Ex-Spouses   204

    Widow(er)s and Surviving Divorced Spouses   204

    Child's Insurance Benefits   206

    Mother's, Father's, and Young Spouse's Benefits   206

    Parent's Benefits   207

Factors That Can Decrease or Increase Benefit Amounts   207

    Actuarial Reduction   207

    Maximum Family Benefits   210

    Pensions Based on Non-Covered Earnings (WEP and GPO)   213

    Working While Receiving Retirement Benefits   217

Wage Income   217

Self-Employment Income   220

Taxation of Benefits   223

Disability Benefits   224

Deeming and Benefit Claiming Strategies   225

When Should You File a Claim for Social Security Retirement Benefits?   226

Filing a Claim for Benefits   229

# About the Editor

jennifer j. rose (jjrose@jjrose.com) was a solo practitioner practicing family law in rural Shenandoah, Iowa, for more than 20 years before moving to Morelia, Michoacán, Mexico, 21 years ago. In that life, she was listed in Best Lawyers in America, rated AV by Martindale-Hubbell, and served a stint as chair of the Iowa State Bar Association Family and Juvenile Law Section.

She served as editor-in-chief of *GPSolo*, the flagship magazine of the American Bar Association General Practice, Solo, and Small Firm Division (now known as the Solo, Small Firm, and General Practice Division), from 1995 to 2007 and again from 2009 until 2011; served on the Division's Council; served as Secretary and Vice Chair of the Division; and served on too many committees and boards to enumerate.

In the ABA Senior Lawyers Division, she serves on its Book Board and Voice of Experience Board.

She has also served terms on the ABA Standing Committee on Continuing Education of the Bar and the Standing Committee on Publishing Oversight. She has served as list manager and den mother for the listserve Solosez, sponsored by the ABA Solo, Small Firm, and General Practice Division, almost since its inception.

She has been a contributing editor to *Matrimonial Strategist* and *Internet Law Researcher*, in addition to having served as a judge of *Law Office Computing*'s annual law firm website competition. She publishes and neglects a blog at redshoesarebetter thanbacon.wordpress.com.

She was editor of the first edition of *How to Capture and Keep Clients* (American Bar Association, 2005) as well as its second edition, published in 2015. She was editor of the first edition of *Effectively Staffing Your Law Firm* (ABA, 2009) as well as its second edition, published in 2017.

# About the Contributors

**DAVID J. ABESHOUSE** is a commercial dispute resolution lawyer concentrating his practice (BizLawNY.com) in business-to-business alternative dispute resolution in Uniondale, Nassau County, New York. David serves as neutral arbitrator on the Commercial Panels of Neutrals of the American Arbitration Association, International Centre for Dispute Resolution, and other ADR forums. He also is a forum-based and private mediator and a trainer of new and experienced mediators and arbitrators. David also serves as a "deal mediator" and as an ADR law consultant to other lawyers. He is a charter member of the New York Academy of Mediators & Arbitrators (NYAMA; Executive Committee Member) and Chapter of the National Academy of Distinguished Neutrals (NADN); he is a Fellow of the College of Commercial Arbitrators (CCA) and a Fellow of the American Bar Foundation (ABF). David is a past adjunct law professor, St. John's University School of Law, teaching ADR Law, and a past chair of the Nassau County Bar Association ADR Law Committee. He has been selected to the New York Metro Area Super Lawyers list for ADR Law for multiple years.

**JEFFREY ALLEN** is a principal in the law firm of Graves & Allen (gravesallen.com), with a general civil practice in California that since 1973 has emphasized negotiation, structuring and documentation of real estate, loan and other business transactions, receiverships, civil litigation, and bankruptcy. He has also worked as an arbitrator since 1975 and a mediator since 1983. In addition to his practice, Jeffrey has been very active in the American

Bar Association, serving on several editorial boards and regularly contributing to several publications. He has also coauthored five books on technology for attorneys. He has had Martindale-Hubbell AV Preeminent rating for nearly 30 consecutive years and was selected as a Northern California Super Lawyer each year from 2014 to 2019. In 2016 the American Bar Association Solo, Small Firm, and General Practice Division gave Jeffrey a Lifetime Achievement Award; in 2017, the Division recognized him for his work as a trainer and educator. He has been semiretired since September 2017.

**JOAN M. BURDA** (jmburda@mac.com) is a solo practitioner (lgbtlaw .com) concentrating in estate planning in Lakewood, Ohio. She is the author of the award-winning book *Estate Planning for Same-Sex Couples*, Third Edition (American Bar Association 2015), as well as *Gay, Lesbian, and Transgender Clients: A Lawyer's Guide* (ABA 2008) and *An Overview of Federal Consumer Law* (ABA 1998)—out of print but a real page-turner. Writing about LGBT legal issues, estate planning, and other topics for various online and print publications, Joan is a featured speaker at national and international conferences and workshops. She is an adjunct professor at Case Western Reserve University School of Law, teaching LGBT Legal Issues and Wills, Trusts, and Future Interests. In her spare time, she reviews books for the *New York Journal of Books*. Joan is a member of the American Bar Association, the Ohio State Bar Association, the National Lesbian and Gay Bar Association, and the American Society of Journalists and Authors.

**MARVIN S.C. DANG** is the managing member of Law Offices of Marvin S.C. Dang, LLLC (marvindanglaw.com) in Honolulu, Hawaii, and has been a lawyer since 1978. He's currently the 2018–2019 Chair of the American Bar Association Senior Lawyers Division, a member of the ABA Nominating Committee, a Delegate in the ABA House of Delegates, and a Commissioner on the ABA Commission on Racial and Ethnic Diversity in the Profession. During the past 42 years, he's held leadership positions in various ABA divisions and sections, beginning with the Law Student Division and continuing with the Young Lawyers Division; the Solo, Small Firm, and General Practice Division; and now the Senior Lawyers Division. A former legislator in the Hawaii State House of Representatives, he's now a registered lobbyist. His law firm's practice areas include legislation, lobbying, creditors' rights, and real estate matters. He received his law degree from the George Washington University Law School in Washington, D.C.

**VICKI LEVY ESKIN**, owner of Levy & Associates, P.A. (levylawyers .com), in Longwood, Florida, focuses her practice on circuit and appellate mediation in addition to her probate, guardianship, and estate practice. She served three years as the National Solo and Small Firm Conference Chair for the American Bar Association Solo, Small Firm, and General Practice Division and served as ABA Advisor to the Uniform Law Commission Committee, drafting the model code addressing fiduciary access to digital assets, and to the parallel committee for the Real Property, Probate, and Trust Law Section of the Florida bar. She has written and lectured on preserving digital assets, international estate planning, and other areas of estate and trust practice and small office management. She is active in local and state bars, serves on several community boards, and mentors other small firm practitioners. Her email address is Vicki@levylawyers.com.

**DAVID R. HAMMER** (davidrhammer45@gmail.com) is a semiretired attorney and a U.S. Coast Guard Mariner Master in Richmond, California. His last full-time employment was from 1998 to 2004 as the County Counsel for Trinity County, California. After four years of pro bono legal and community services, David returned to part-time public employment, representing Trinity County Child Protective Services. Prior to his public employment, he was a sole practitioner for 23 years. David believes that lawyers have a duty to provide public service. He was the pro bono lawyer for the Weaverville Volunteer Fire Department; chairman of the County Drug and Substance Prevention Advisory Board; chairman of the Juvenile Justice and Delinquency Prevention Commission; delegate to the State Bar Convention; past president of two Rotary clubs; and chairman of several Rotary District committees for Northern California. He is now a licensed boat captain and teaches sailing on San Francisco Bay.

**VICTORIA L. HERRING** (victoriaherring@mac.com) practiced civil rights, discrimination, and employment law in Des Moines, Iowa, as Division Head of the Civil Rights Division of the Iowa Attorney General's office, with a law firm, and as a solo practitioner. As she moved to part-time practice, her love of photography made her a fine art, architectural, and travel photographer, whose work has been displayed throughout the Midwest. Her foray into a second act began with JourneyZing, which provides customized travel research and planning for domestic and international venues and photographic fine art (gallery.JourneyZing.com), which led her to becoming a founding partner and manager of the upscale Artisan Gallery 218 (artisangallery218.com) in the historic Valley Junction of West Des Moines, Iowa. She is the longtime columnist Mac User for *GPSolo* magazine and a member of the Board of Trustees of Des Moines University.

**DAVID ZACHARY KAUFMAN** (david@businessbrawls.com) started law school at the GMU School of Law (now Scalia Law School) when he was 40 years old. Graduating in 1991, he worked briefly at a large law firm and then went out on his own in 1996, founding the litigation firm that eventually became the Kaufman Law Group, PLLC. David has been an adjunct professor of law at George Mason University School of Law and has practiced various forms of martial arts for over 55 years. As he winds down his litigation practice, he has increasingly been asked to testify as an expert witness in criminal and civil cases. He is the author of Qui Custodes, a blog of self-defense, 101 Personal Protection Tips, 101 Business Protection Tips, and "Workplace Security for Solo and Small Firm Staff," a chapter in the American Bar Association book *Effectively Staffing Your Law Firm*. David also teaches several CLE/LPM classes each year on law firm security. A member of the Washington, D.C., Maryland, and Virginia bars, he now lives in Sarasota, Florida.

**WENDY LASCHER** (wlascher@fcoplaw.com), a Southern California native, earned her JD at the University of Michigan Law School in 1973. She was hired by the late Edward Lascher. They became law partners in 1978 and married two years later. After his death in 1991, Wendy continued practicing law in their Victorian building in downtown Ventura. In 2011, she became a partner at Ferguson Case Orr Paterson, LLP. Wendy handles appeals throughout California and beyond. She has represented clients before the United States Supreme Court, the California Supreme Court, and multiple U.S. Circuit Courts of Appeal and in every California Court of Appeal district. She has also handled cases in state and federal trial courts—and advised many potential clients not to appeal. Wendy frequently speaks to lawyers about making the record for appeal, legal writing, and handling writs and appeals.

**DAVID J. LEFFLER** (DLeffler@culhanemeadows.com) has worked for over 30 years with small businesses, many technology-based, in a variety of industries. He has advised them on formation issues, contract negotiations, and the structuring of asset acquisitions and often fulfills the role of outside general counsel. David has been honored as a Super Lawyer in the fields of corporate, intellectual property, and real estate law for the years 2014–2018. For ten years ending in 2012, he wrote a column on law practice management for solo attorneys for the American Bar Association's

*GPSolo* magazine. He has served on advisory boards and from 2011 through 2015 as a judge for the New York StartUP! Business Plan Competition, which is sponsored by Citi Foundation and is held at the Science, Industry, and Business Library of the New York Public Library. David received his law degree from the Benjamin Cardozo School of Law in 1981. After a lifetime in New York City, he recently relocated to Austin, Texas.

**SCOTT R. MOTE** (Smote@Ohiolap.org) of Columbus, Ohio, is Executive Director of the Ohio Lawyers Assistance Program, Inc. (OLAP). Before making OLAP a full-time endeavor, he practiced law in Columbus for 30 years, the last 18 as founding partner of Harris, McClellan, Binau & Cox PLL. He has served on the American Bar Association Commission on Lawyer Assistance Programs (Commissioner, 2010–2013); Ohio State Bar Association Council of Delegates, the Estate Planning & Probate Law Section, and the Lawyers Assistance Committee; the Florida Bar's Out-of-State Practitioners Division; the Columbus Bar Association (Admissions (Chair 1994–1996), Probate Committees); Ohio State Bar Foundation; Columbus Bar Foundation; Central Ohio Association for Justice; Franklin County Trial Lawyers Association; and the Central Ohio Association of Criminal Defense Lawyers. He has received the Columbus Bar Association's 2005 award of merit for service to the profession; the Ohio State Bar Association's 2006 Ohio Bar Medal, its highest award for service to the profession; the Ohio State Bar Association's 2010 Eugene R. Weir Award for Ethics and Professionalism; and Capital University Law School's 2013 alumni of the year award.

**LISA A. RUNQUIST** (runquist.com) of Northridge, California, has represented nonprofits for over 40 years. She has authored numerous publications on nonprofits, including authoring and editing *Guide to Representing Religious Organizations* (2009) and authoring *The ABCs of Nonprofits* (2nd ed. 2015), which is also now available in Spanish: *El ABC de Law Organizaciones Sin Fines de Lucro*. Lisa was the first winner of the Outstanding Lawyer Award, an American Bar Association Business Law Section Nonprofit Lawyers Award, and in 2010 the first person to also win the Vanguard Award for lifetime achievement. She is a member and former chair of the ABA BLS Nonprofit Organizations Committee and the California Lawyers Association Nonprofit Organizations Committee, served on the editorial board of *Business Law Today*, serves as an Editorial Advisor for ChurchLawAndTax.com, and is an adjunct professor at Trinity Law School.

**AVRAM L. SACKS** (avram@asackslaw.com) is an attorney in private practice in Skokie, Illinois, concentrating on Social Security law and benefits. He is a former Assistant Regional Counsel for the Social Security Administration, past editor of the *CCH Social Security Law Reporter*, founding member of the Special Needs Alliance advisory council, and the author of two books on Social Security law. A member of the National Academy of Elder Law Attorneys and the National Organization of Social Security Claimants' Representatives, Avram frequently lectures on Social Security matters. In addition to successfully representing clients in cases before the U.S. District Court for the Northern District of Illinois and the U.S. Sixth and Seventh Circuit Courts of Appeal, Avram advises clients on how to maximize their Social Security retirement benefits through optimal claiming strategies.

**CRAIG A. STOKES** (cstokes@stokeslawoffice.com) is a founding partner of the eponymous law firm, based in San Antonio, Texas. He is admitted to practice in Texas, Florida, California, Arizona, Pennsylvania, New York, Missouri, Oklahoma, Iowa, Minnesota, Oregon, South Dakota, Utah, Idaho, North Carolina, Virginia, New Jersey, New Hampshire, Massachusetts, Georgia, Alabama, Mississippi, West Virginia, Alaska, Tennessee, Kentucky, Rhode Island, and Washington and is admitted to practice before various federal district and appellate courts, including the United States District Courts of Connecticut, Illinois, Indiana, Michigan, Colorado, Vermont, and Puerto Rico. He passed his first bar exam in Iowa in January 1981, when the bar exam, revelation of results, and swearing in all took place in a single week. Craig's practice is largely in agricultural law. He and some of his colleagues have been referred to as members of the "broccoli bar." *Kingdom Fresh Produce, Inc. v. Stokes Law Office*, LLP, 845 F.3d 609, 621 n.6 (5th Cir. 2016).

**JIMMY VERNER** of Dallas, Texas (jverner101@vernerlegal.com), received his JD in 1979 from the University of San Diego, where he served as executive editor of the *San Diego Law Review*. After graduation, Jimmy clerked for a federal district court judge in Mississippi, subsequently relocating to Memphis to spend three years in a general practice. Jimmy He later moved to Dallas, where he practiced commercial litigation and later family law. He is board certified in Civil Trial Law and Family Law by the Texas Board of Legal Specialization. Jimmy eventually focused his practice on family law appellate work but in the meantime earned his PhD in Public Policy and Political Economy. Since 2015, after attending an inspirational seminar, he has assisted startups in entity selection and formation, especially with respect to social enterprises. He works mostly online at home part-time but comes off the bench as needed by his firm, Verner Brumley Mueller & Parker PC.

**TED A. WAGGONER** practices in a small firm, Peterson & Waggoner, LLP (peterson-waggoner.com), in Rochester, Indiana. A general practitioner with an emphasis on real estate, estate planning, and business issues, Ted has focused on business planning concerns for a variety of clients and is a civil mediator. He is active with the Indiana State Bar Association and the Indiana Bar Foundation, where he serves as Chair of the Fellows. Ted is a Fellow of the American Bar Foundation.

**ROBIN PAGE WEST** was studying photojournalism in college when the events of Watergate inspired her to go to law school. After a stint at her state attorney general's office and several years as a litigator at small and medium-size firms, she hung out her solo shingle and developed a successful niche: federal Civil False Claims Act practice. She went on to become the Editor-in-Chief of the American Bar Association Litigation Section's flagship publication, *Litigation*, and to author the ABA book *Advising the Qui Tam Whistleblower: From Identifying a Case to Filing under the False Claims Act* (2d ed. 2009). She continued to represent whistleblowers with knowledge of fraud on the government until relocating to Austin, Texas, where she is planning an ambitious garden and pursuing a new phase in life.

# About This Book

*jennifer j. rose*

This book is dedicated to all of those lawyers, and particularly solo and small firm lawyers, who have reached (or are approaching) the realization that they've got fewer years ahead of them than behind. Many have practiced law longer than they've done anything else in their lives. And for some, the tenure of their practice may only seem like a life sentence.

Today's senior lawyers remember where they were when Kennedy was shot and what they were doing when the *Challenger* exploded, and they recognize that Haldeman, Ehrlichman, Mitchell, and Dean was not a District of Columbia law firm.

The 1970s were marked by greater numbers than ever attending law school, eventually passing the bar, and embarking upon legal careers. In 1980, the number of lawyers with active bar licenses increased a whopping 15.4 percent over the year before. Now 574,810 lawyers were available to serve a country populated by 226,545,805 souls; 0.25 percent of the population were lawyers. By 2018, the ranks of actively practicing lawyers would swell to 1,338,678, or 0.41 percent of the population (https://www.americanbar.org/news/abanews/aba-news-archives/2018/05/new_aba_data_reveals/). The need for legal services didn't grow accordingly, and solo and small firm lawyers' incomes dropped after being adjusted for inflation. A lot more lawyers were demanding a slice of the pie.

Let's go back to that great mass of lawyers who started out in 1980. Those who were age 25 then are on the brink of eligibility for Medicare. Some are still plying the profession, some are already receiving Social Security benefits, and some are contemplating what their next move should be.

More lawyers than ever are at retirement age, and, at the same time, retirement takes on hues not envisioned by our fathers' generations. Lawyers may leave the practice, but their skills, attitudes, and approaches bring different perspectives to lives beyond the law office.

How do you know when it's time to leave? How do you pare down a practice to part-time? How does a small firm move a partner who can no longer perform out of the practice? What are the options for a lawyer who's just hit his or her late 50s or early 60s and who wants out? What employment options exist for those who don't have comfortable retirement plans but who really want, and possibly need, to get out of the practice? And, what does a lawyer do after leaving the practice?

Second acts are more frequent. It's not all about shuffleboard, mahjong, and golf. It's not about grandchildren and moving to The Villages. Some second acts are for the money, because there's not enough money to go around. Sometimes the money is necessary to maintain a lifestyle, to supplement a pension and Social Security. Sometimes it's just to pay for the better things in life, and sometimes the money generated from a second career is just gravy. Some second acts are natural extensions of hobbies developed while in practice. Some second acts aren't learned until the law practice is closed up for good. And some second acts are nothing more than doing something just for the fun of it. And some really are related to the practice of law, leveraging those skills built up over the years, putting those talents to different uses.

The idea for this book came out of conversations over the past decade with a friend I'll call Brad, even though that's not his real name. Unless you count that summer as a camp counselor, Brad, now 64, has never done anything but practice law. After his almost four decades as a lawyer, he is very well respected, rated one of the Best Lawyers in America, decked with all of those badges of honor heaped upon the most successful in his area of practice, writing and speaking on serious topics of substantive law, and consulted on pending legislation, but he's no longer the star he once was. He has the money to comfortably provide for himself, but he doesn't know what he'd do if he weren't practicing law. An appointment to the bench could lead to exiting the practice, but after being turned down three times, that's not likely to happen. His tenure may mean that he can practice more efficiently, but he's no longer as quick on his feet as he once was, he's been the target of a complaint from the bar disciplinary folks, there was that hint of a malpractice claim, and he was even assaulted at the courthouse by some crazy person. Asked when he's going to retire, he'll readily come back with the desire to take a case to the U.S. Supreme Court. Just once, and he thinks he has something that's headed that way. Maybe in another decade. It's not going to happen.

"I could be one of those lawyers who's still practicing at the age of 95," he insists, never mind that octogenarians didn't run in his family. His service dog and handicapped license plate don't create a picture of health.

"You're a solo, practicing with one secretary, and no spouse or progeny waiting in the wings to lend succor," I tell him. That's not exactly the kind of team most still-practicing, outlier 95-year-old lawyers might have. Brad admits that keeling over while writing a brief on a Sunday night might not be a bad way to go.

You're still a lawyer, even if you're no longer practicing, I remind him. He could still go to bar association meetings, serve on bar association committees, and speak at continuing legal education programs. He could become an adjunct professor, and he could volunteer at legal aid if he wanted.

Or he could do none of the above, and just enjoy his dog, the never-ending hunt for gourmet foods and fine wine, and his boat. And if he really needed to legitimize his departure from practicing law, he could call all of that his second act.

"But I like driving up to my office and seeing my name on that shingle."

There are some battles you just can't win. Brad, this book is for you. Please read it and start on your second act.

The lawyers who contributed to this book come from a broad range of practice settings and styles in big cities and small towns. Some are just barely 60, and some have already celebrated their 70th birthdays and beyond. Some have already left the practice of law, some are only recently retired, some teach and consult, and some are still toiling in the grassy pastures. Each has had hands-on, practical experience owning and operating a solo or small law firm, and each has shared his or her expertise generously in the development of this book.

This book would not have been possible without the friendship, guidance, and leadership of Chuck Collier, Marvin S.C. Dang, Seth Rosner, Jeffrey M. Allen, the entire Senior Lawyers Division Book Board, Sarah Craig, Lorraine Murray, Emily Roschek, Lexie Heinemann, and Bryan Kay.

And, of course, nothing would be possible without the constant presence of Morgen Rose.

# Part I

# Deciding When It's Time to Leave

Should I stay or should I go? That question trips up many lawyers, who'll invest hours, months, and years trying to settle on the right answer. And for most, the best answer is the one that makes them feel the most comfortable. It's not a decision to be made lightly, but at the same time, lawyers really shouldn't spend more time pondering what to do than they invested in getting that law degree and passing the bar exam.

**Chapter 1**

Time to Retire
*Robin Page West*

**Chapter 2**

A Five-Year Plan for Active Retirement
*David Zachary Kaufman*

**Chapter 3**

You've Got Options, Lots and Lots and Lots of Options!
*Jeffrey Allen*

**Chapter 4**

A Nontraditional Law Firm Provides a Roadmap for Your
Transition to Retirement
*David J. Leffler*

**Chapter 5**

Scaling Back a Practice to Part-Time, Winding Down, and
Changing Practice Specialties and Practice Styles
*Robin Page West*

# 1

## Time to Retire

### by Robin Page West

When is it time to retire? I vacillated a lot on that over the course of my career, depending on how events of the moment were playing out. When my practice was humming along making good money and the cases I was working on were interesting and challenging, I expected to work up until the end just like *L.A. Law*'s senior partner Norman Chaney, who was found dead at his desk, nose in a plate of food, during the pilot episode. (I didn't actually know of any real women lawyers who had worked until their deaths, but in 2018 I read the obituary of Cravath's first female partner, Christine Beshar, who died at 88, officially retired but still practicing. So perhaps the fantasy was not all that far-fetched.)

Other times, such as when judges failed to understand the most basic issues in a motion or sided with the opposition and thwarted my strategy, I railed against the system and vowed to find something better to do with my time, right away. But if I could turn things around and regain my footing, my attitude toward the profession would usually improve and I'd be back for another round of litigation insanity.

When large contingent fee settlements seemed like real possibilities, I daydreamed about expanding my practice and hiring more staff to take some of the pressure off. At the same time, though, I also longed to leave the lawyer's fog of deadlines, conflict, and responsibilities in search of a gentler, happier daily energy.

After a few decades of the highs and lows of litigation practice, heartburn took away the joy of eating, and cascades of cortisol rendered me so nervous I jumped every time the phone rang. Maybe if I had been better at meditating, things wouldn't have gotten to that point. But since everyone else in the office was on blood pressure medication and/or antidepressants, I considered myself to be holding up well under the circumstances. Even so, I knew taking a break would be good for me, so I decided to accompany my then-15-year-old daughter on a year of school abroad to calm my nerves. There, I settled into a new environment that included a bunch of happily retired expats.

I cut my work hours way back and watched them spend their days leisurely doing errands, tending their gardens, going to cultural events, museums and gallery openings, building additions on their homes, making art and music, doing charitable work, cooking, reading, and basically just doing whatever they felt like.

I started comparing their lives to mine. Could I do that, too? Could I spend as much time as I wanted learning to cook? My inner voice was telling me no, I had to stay on my current path. My practice was the best it had ever been; I shouldn't squander it. That even if I thought I could afford to walk away from it, I might be wrong. I should do more to give back to the profession. My work kept me mentally sharp. My friends back home were still working, so I shouldn't stop until some of them did. My whole life since college had been devoted to becoming a lawyer, being a lawyer, and then to becoming a better lawyer. It's who I am, and I'm very good at it; why would I stop?

After my year abroad was up, I noticed my heartburn was gone and I felt much less stressed. I didn't really want to go back to work full-time, but I didn't have any other path mapped out. My inner voice had given me sufficient reasons not to retire. The idea that I could stop being a lawyer or change my pursuits seemed impossible. But still, the seed had been planted. I didn't want the heartburn to come back.

The same thing happened to former Maryland Attorney General Stephen H. Sachs when he took a six-month sabbatical to France while a partner at what was then Wilmer, Cutler & Pickering. In an interview by Douglas D. Connah, Jr., published in the Summer 2001 issue of *Experience* magazine, Sachs was asked, "Did that sabbatical influence your decision to retire?" Sachs responded,

> It's very close to the heart of the matter. I'd never had anything even remotely resembling a sabbatical before, and what it really did underscore for me was what I knew intellectually but had never really experienced, and that is that there's a whole world out there. Fill in the blanks. It's difficult to talk about this without clichés, but the idea that I could grow in other ways than just as a lawyer was palpable.

Connah, a former Venable partner now in hot pursuit of what he calls the "unforgettable highs" of performing onstage as a musician in a big band, described his own such growth in a Summer 2000 article in that same magazine entitled "Music in My Ears":

> I had already graduated (I prefer that term to retired) from the practice of law and had discovered that performing music in bands or for audiences was itself abundantly stress-producing. The little knot that now rises in my stomach while driving to rehearsal or waiting to go onstage feels just like the one that once formed as I walked to the courthouse. I've concluded that a modest level of stress is not just inevitable, but also, at least for me, a necessary part of keeping the edges sharp. I see it as something to pursue, not avoid.

Whether it be as a result of a sabbatical, a desire to pursue another life-long love, or even an ordinary daydream, once the possibility of moving into that other world takes root, more issues arise. Does one have, or want, an identity outside of being a lawyer? Is everything accomplished in the lawyer realm, or must some unfinished business be completed? How important is it to control the timing of one's own retirement? Should the urge for growth in a different direction and the potential to control one's own calendar be put on hold, or is now the time? And finally, even though the calculators and spreadsheets may seem to confirm financial independence, what about that little voice that continues to urge "strive for more"?

As a young associate, my hobbies, recreational activities, social life, and even the needs of my houseplants and pet cat were eclipsed by the demands of my job. The partners I reported to were of exactly the same mind as Florida Super Lawyer Lee Stapleton, who wrote this in her acclaimed essay "I Don't Feel Your Pain: A Partner's View of Associates," *Litigation*, Vol. 39, No. 2, Summer 2013:

> First of all, do realize that being an associate is not a journey of personal discovery—it's a job with partners and clients who have a great number of expectations and generally not that much patience. I am constantly amazed when associates talk to me very sincerely about their personal growth and what's on their life's bucket list. . . . I truly wish you a well-rounded life, but your rounding off must work within the straight lines that are the parameters of lawyering.

Sounds harsh, but alas, for many of us, that was our reality. Having stayed within the parameters of lawyering for decades meant we gave up the possibility of other pursuits that might have also given our life meaning, sometimes to the exclusion of all interests not related to work. Others may have managed successfully to pursue and maintain connections to life outside the straight lines. Which are you? If the former, leaving the law may find you facing a vast emptiness and nothing to do with your time. Without the accomplishments of the workday to reflect upon, you may feel you have nothing to offer, no one to advise, help, mentor. Should you be hesitant to retire because of concerns like these, consider finding some activities or cultivating some relationships outside your practice before retiring. Let these expand to take up a significant amount of your time, so that when you do decide to step away from work, you have a soft place to land.

Timing is important. Since lawyers usually have multiple projects going all at the same time, stopping cold turkey usually is not the best option if one has a choice. Gradually tapering off might work better, for example, by ceasing to take new cases but continuing to work on the ones already undertaken. Another factor to consider in the timing of retirement is the way the political winds are blowing in your firm or office. Are you concerned someone may be getting ready to make a grab for your power or change the structure within which you operate? Try to undermine you? Change the compensation formula? Reshuffle the secretary and paralegal assignments? Is the firm about to move offices? If you can foresee any events on the horizon that could be annoying or unpleasant, you can plan to be gone by then. Similarly, if you have any disciplinary, ethical, or substance abuse inquiries pending against you, consider whether exiting the practice might be a satisfactory way to resolve them.

Then there's the issue of whether you are really emotionally finished with being a lawyer. Are you satisfied with what you've accomplished? Is there something you always wanted to do, perhaps argue in a certain court or settle a case for an amount over a certain dollar figure, that is within striking distance right now? Such a goal can be an excellent touchstone for closing down a practice and moving on in a different direction. Simply decide that when that goal—closing your largest client's last retail lease in the shopping center or settling Mrs. X's malpractice case—is attained, then you will stop. Moving on to a new life makes sense when you've finished the old one on a high note.

One of my most persistent conundrums was whether I had enough money to last as long as I needed it to, and making matters more difficult was the fact that, of course, I did not know how long that would be. I started following blogger Sydney Lagier, an accountant who retired just before the 2008 recession at age 44 with a 70% allocation to stock mutual funds and 30% allocation to bond funds and cash. She survived it and shared her strategy for determining whether a portfolio is robust enough to retire in her blog post "How Much Money Do You Need to Retire?" (https://retiredsyd.typepad.com/retirement_a_fulltime_job/2008/08/how-much-money-do-you-need-to-retire.html):

1.  [Divide your current nest egg] by your living expenses that will not be covered by other income sources such as Social Security or pensions. If you are 65 years old, that number should be right around 25. The larger it is, the better shape you are in. That represents how many years' living expenses you have before accounting for inflation and earnings on that nest egg. History shows that should take you no less than 33 years through retirement, even if our markets experience markets matching the worst 33 years in the last century.

2.  Now, take a look at your stable liquid assets—cash, CDs, short-term bond funds. Divide that number by your living expenses that will not be covered by other income sources. As a point of reference, it took the stock market almost seven years to reach the peak level it achieved in 2007 before the recession. Do you have enough to live on if it takes that long again or will you be forced to sell some of your stocks at huge discounts to keep your head above water? Any stock you sell at the bottom represents gains you will never see again when the market goes back up. You've made those losses permanent.

3.  Take your portfolio and multiply the equity side of it by 46%. Now subtract that number from your total portfolio. Divide the result by your annual expenses not covered by other sources. How different is that than the number you came up with in #1—the one that was hopefully around 25? Try one more thing. Divide this reduced portfolio by

the number you came up with in #1. Can you figure out a way to live on the resulting number instead of the number you were counting on?

4.  Historically, if you retired with 25 times your expenses at age 65, you'd likely be ok even without adjusting your spending. But how does the hypothetical situation in #3 FEEL to you? Doesn't it make you FEEL like making some cutbacks? It made me feel like cutting back expenses in 2008 (and 2009 and 2010!).

The first time I read that post, I had no idea what she was saying. But after following it step by step, and doing the calculations, I not only understood but felt confident that I knew the parameters of what my portfolio could withstand and could predict how bad things would be if the market were to drop precipitously. There's an element of uncertainty, as in many things, but it's not rocket science.

In addition to Sidney's formulas, I tried some of the ubiquitous online retirement calculators. One in particular caught my eye: https://www.firecalc.com/. It bills itself as "FIRECalc: a different kind of retirement calculator." "FIRE" stands for "financially independent, retire early." The calculator looks at investment returns and analyzes what would have happened if you retired in 1871, 1872, 1873, and each succeeding year and tells you how often your strategy would have succeeded historically (meaning you died before your portfolio was depleted). It also lets you plug in different spending amounts, inflation rates, portfolio allocations, and other variables, allowing you to catastrophize to your heart's content and then see what it means in terms of dollars decades hence.

While tinkering with FIRECalc, I noticed the same site also hosts a forum of people who are retired or planning to be. I started lurking and soon got addicted to this online soap opera of real people focused on money issues in retirement. To be sure, there are many online forums on investing, money matters, and retirement, but this is the one I got involved with by happenstance. I was a fly on the wall seeing the mundane details of the posters' lives: how they saved, spent, and invested money; how they relished not needing an alarm clock; whether they believed in market timing or set-and-forget index funds. Soon-to-be retirees, often categorized as "class of 2025," etc. would seek advice from the long-retireds who are pleased to share their own personal stories. Ten or fifteen minutes a day reading what people living the much-coveted retired lifestyle had to say made me feel like I wanted it, too. Once again, I found myself rubbing elbows with the happily-retireds, this time not abroad, but virtually. I was getting excited about becoming one myself.

I knew I was ready to go in a different direction. I had no fear I would not be busy with scores of things I had been wanting to do for a long time. Being a lawyer did not define me, and in fact I usually avoid talking about it when with friends or meeting new people anyway. And my calculations and spreadsheets were telling me I was good to go. The one thing still giving me pause was the concern that regardless, I should keep working to earn more. The idea was ingrained and hard to shake.

Then I read the short story "How Much Land Does a Man Need?" by Leo Tolstoy. Although the wife of the protagonist is happy to live a peasant's life, her husband is not. He is consumed by an overwhelming desire to acquire more and more land by dint of hard work, planning, and follow-through. Despite his success, he still wants more and is finally offered all the land he can circumnavigate on foot in a single day. Unfortunately, he overestimates how far and how quickly he can walk and dies from exertion just as he arrives at the finish line, where he is unceremoniously buried in a six-foot grave—all the land he needed.

Message received. Thank you, Mr. Tolstoy.

# 2

# A Five-Year Plan for Active Retirement

*by David Zachary Kaufman*

## Introduction

If you are reading this, CONGRATULATIONS! You have decided to retire in the near future. Or maybe you have already retired. Or (best of all) you see the writing on the wall and have decided that it is time to start planning to retire. I'm 70. I just retired. But I've been planning for this retirement for about five years—since I was 65 and went on Medicare. You should too—even better, start earlier . . . the earlier the better.

Why did I decide to retire? After all, I feel pretty good. I'm in good health other than a few kinetic injuries from a very active youth that have caught up with me. I've been successful at law and have been doing high-stakes litigation for over 25 years—22 of them as either a sole practitioner or as the managing director of a small firm. But it's time.

How did I know it was time to retire? When every day brought more stress, not more delight and joy. My children are grown and fully launched—no dependents other than the puppy. So, my only obligations were to myself. And I wanted more from my life. I had things to do, places to visit, and enjoyment to find again.

Once I came to this realization, I had to decide what I wanted—not what I did not want. This article describes that five-year journey.

# Who Am I? Who Is "Me"?

To understand my journey, to apply it to your own experiences, you should know something about me. I went to law school 30 years ago, when I was 40 years old. This was, at the time, an unheard-of decision. But I did it. Then I spent all my career doing litigation—mostly bespoke litigation for entrepreneurs and owner-managed companies, usually no more than four to six cases at any one time. I was always either solo or, later, in a small firm, the Kaufman Law Group, of no more than three lawyers plus staff—I always tried to be as lean as possible.

In addition, to combat the stress of litigation, I continued with my other avocation: the martial arts. Since 1964 I have studied and trained (almost every day unless I was in trial) in various martial arts including kendo, iaido, karate, judo, jiujitsu, Tang Soo Do, and others. Partly as fallout from this experience, and partly as fallout from the work I did before going to law school, I have also provided personal and professional security consultation advice and services.

But when I turned 65, I realized that the time was coming when I would not relish the adrenaline charge of high-stakes litigation. On the other hand, I knew myself well enough to know that I loved the law and hated the idea of being a "retired lawyer" who just goes to meetings and drones on about the old days. I knew I would always want to be physically and mentally active. I knew I had to create a plan for the future.

I turned 70 this year and retired (mostly) from litigation. After living in Virginia for 40 years, I moved to Florida. Here are the questions I asked, my own answers, and the plans I made as a result. Overall the plan took three to five years to put together and implement.

# What Did I Want from "Retirement"?

What was the "retirement" I wanted? When I started this process, I didn't know. But I knew what I didn't want: I did not want to retire and just sit around waiting to die. I did not want my brain to atrophy. When I visited Florida's retirement communities, I saw too many people who seemed to me to have stopped growing mentally and physically, to be just waiting to die. I did not want to be like that. Golf, bridge, mahjong, and early bird specials were not interesting—at least not to me.

I wanted to be involved in the world; I wanted to be engaged and engaging. Even though I did not want to litigate cases anymore, I wanted to stay involved in the law—something I loved. I wanted to be physically active as much as I could, to push my limits. I wanted to enjoy life, to do things because I wanted to do them, not because I had a duty or obligation.

# Implementation

This was not the first time I had confronted a major change in my life—after all, I totally turned my life around and went to law school at age 40 with a wife, a baby, and a large mortgage. This change would be easier—I hoped.

## Stay or Go? Where to Live

According to the AARP, about 90% of people over 65 want to retire in place and live in their own homes for as long as they can. That wouldn't work for me. Where to live after retirement was a big question for me. I had lived in Virginia for over 30 years when I started planning to retire. My network of friends and acquaintances was in Virginia. My practice was Virginia-based, even though I was also admitted in Maryland and the District of Columbia. My home was in Virginia—I still lived in the too-large house where my daughters had grown up even though they were long gone.

But I started to think. Where were my daughters living? One married into the military and moves regularly—they are in Japan right now but will be reassigned to another base within two years. The other had moved to Jerusalem, had married, and would not be returning—their home is there now. Both had their own homes—mine was now up to me. I also began to realize that the stress of living in a D.C. suburb in Virginia was high. Between traffic, crowding, and other stressors, just living in Northern Virginia's fast-paced environment was an adrenaline-charged adventure. I realized I was exhausted and wanted a slower pace to my life. So, what did I want? Where did I want to go?

My needs, wants, and desires drove my decision.

I decided I had two needs: close access to a major international airport so I could get to my daughters quickly (or as quickly as possible given the distances involved) and affordability. As I began to search, a third and fourth factor surfaced: I wanted to find a place with good medical care and a friendly, low-stress environment where, as a Jew, I could feel accepted.

With these needs, wants, and desires carefully in mind I continued the search. There were no constraints on the search. I looked at New Mexico, Colorado, Louisiana, other parts of Virginia, North Carolina, Atlanta, and Florida. I ruled out Colorado because I was sick of shoveling snow. I loved Santa Fe but decided that it was too hard to get to the airport in Albuquerque. Richmond and Williamsburg, Virginia, were very tempting indeed, and I spent a lot of time investigating them before I eventually decided that those venues would not work for me. Finally, and completely aware that I was acting out a cliché, I looked at Florida. It turns out that Florida is actually four states in one: Miami, Orlando, Tampa, and Pensacola. Each is very different from the others. I fell in love with the area south of Tampa and decided to move there. It was close to Tampa's international airport and was affordable. There was good medical care available. Finally, I found a wonderful, accepting environment that welcomed me with open arms.

## When to Retire Is Up to You

The first thing I had to do as I started to plan for my retirement was to confront a key question: When to retire? After all, I needed to have some idea of how much time I had to plan and prepare. There is a plethora of books advising people on when to retire. The American Bar Association has several of them specifically designed for lawyers. So did my local library. I got a bunch of them and read them. Amazingly, none agreed. Depending on which authority you follow, you should not retire until you cannot work any longer. Or you should retire as soon as you can afford to. (But nobody tells you how to do that.) Or you should retire when you first become eligible for Social Security. Or you should wait until your Social Security annuity is maximized.

## When to Retire Depends on Your Financial Situation

### *Your Future Lifestyle Will Determine Your Financial Needs*

Do your children have special needs? Any needs you will have to supplement? What about grandchildren? Do they have needs you want to provide for? On a personal note, how big a house do you need? Will you need servants? Do you need more than one house—a vacation home, for example? Do you want to become what Floridians call a "snowbird"? Will you live in your original home over the summer and move to Florida from November to May? Or will you downsize to a simpler life? Maybe live full-time in your vacation home? Or something else? Do you have a bucket list? Do you wish to travel? How often? First class? Primitive? Luxury hotels? Hostels? Safaris come in all price tags too. You will need some pretty good answers to these questions, as they will affect your annual expenses and therefore how much money you have to put aside. If you have a life partner, be sure to consult them too—their ideas may (probably will) differ from yours. Surprises in this area can be very unpleasant. Check first and be sure everyone's interests are taken into account.

### *Your Financial Needs Depend on Your Expected Life Span*

You might have noticed that much of the advice you get on when to retire depends on money. Unstated, but real, is another variable—your expected life span. You will have to make some educated guesses about how long you can expect to live in order to make some of these decisions. It's not easy either. For example, I had to consider how long my father lived (70), how long my mother lived (90), my assorted kinetic injuries (foot, legs, chest, shoulder), my lifestyle (gym four to six times a week), eating habits, and the assorted life expectancy tables available online. After consideration I decided that planning on a life expectancy of 90 was probably close.

### *Your Financial Needs Depend on Your Mental and Physical Fitness*

Then I had to estimate how long I might be able to maintain an active lifestyle, versus merely being alive. Based on very little fact, I decided that I should plan on having about five years of slowly declining health but for about 15 years I would be able to have an active lifestyle. All my parents and grandparents (so far as I knew) had maintained their faculties until their deaths, so I decided not to be worried about adult onset dementia or Alzheimer's disease.

In sum, I decided that I should plan for 15 years of physically active retirement (e.g., travel, etc.) and about five years of declining—but still mentally active—health. So, I needed to have enough financial resources to live the life I wanted for 20 years, 15 of them very active years.

## Your Life Experiences and Fitness Will Control What to Do during Your Active Life

### *Deal with Physical Issues First*

Initially I had to deal with a physical problem: You see, my legs had been damaged by kinetic injuries. When I was 65 I could not walk 100 yards, even with a cane. Two years later, after significant surgery, I spent 15 days hiking in the Himalayas. Three years after that, I could barely walk 20,000 steps even with steel braces. It was agonizing. So, I had to get my knees fixed. I've done that now and am striving toward a goal of being able to walk ten miles carrying a 25-pound backpack. I'm not there yet, but I expect to be by next spring. Once that was dealt with (or the plan to deal with these injuries was put in place), I was able to start planning for my active retirement.

## Look Back to Walk Forward

My first step in deciding what to do with my life was to look backward. That's right—to go forward I had to look back. What did I enjoy doing now? What did I enjoy before my injuries became incapacitating? What new things did I want to learn? The answers turned out to be interesting.

First, I went back to riding motorcycles. I had ridden for years, but when my girls were born I was told/decided that it was too dangerous to ride in the urban area where I was working. So, I sold my bike. Now I was ready to ride again. But I did not just buy a motorcycle and start riding. This time I took classes. I joined a club. I pestered more experienced riders for tips. It turns out that simply riding a big (1200-pound) motorcycle can be physically demanding. At least, I had trouble riding long distances (100–200 miles) without a break.

Second, I love to travel and walk, and I used to love hiking and backpacking, especially with my Newfoundland dog Andy. I wanted to do all those things again. So, I created a bucket list of places to visit and things to do. For example, I want to visit every national park in the continental United States. I also want to visit the Parthenon, climb the pyramids, do a photo safari in Zimbabwe, dive the Great Barrier Reef, and—bless and keep me—attend the gladiator school that is in Rome.

Third, ever since June 1964 I have studied and trained in the martial arts. They are part of my life. Now that I'm older I can no longer fight—but I still study them, even though I had to stop training about a year ago when my physical limitations finally caught up with me. Now I'm getting back into shape and expect to start training again next year.

Fourth, I want to learn new things. I want to take a class in sailing and maybe get my certificate. I want to scuba again, so I need to learn the new techniques.

## Strangely Enough, I Still Love the Law

Unlike many of my lawyer friends, perhaps because they went to law school straight out of college and I went later in life, I do not wish to disengage from the law. I merely wish to find a new way to be engaged. But how? Did I want to do pro bono work? Did I want to teach? Research and write? What did I really want to do? Again, I had to look back to move forward. I realized that I loved the subtleties and arguments in the law. I loved researching esoteric questions. Most of all, though, I loved standing up to bullies.

BINGO! I realized what I wanted to do with my future life. Not only that, I realized that I could combine my passions for law and the martial arts into one project. I would become an expert witness on personal security and the use of force by police and anyone else. I decided I would also work to develop an expertise in 4th Amendment law. Maybe, I told myself, I would even do some pro bono work helping other lawyers.

Now I admit that it took me over a year to figure this out. And to some extent it was serendipity—another lawyer who knew me called me to ask about testifying as an expert martial artist. Just about then another man I knew called me to ask me to put together a group of martial artists to teach special techniques to a group of U.S. military special operators. I did so and they were all impressed. OKAY! I only have to be hit with a hammer so many times before I get the idea.

## Planning for the Future Career Is Critical

Now I needed a plan to develop a reputation as an expert. So, I researched what an "expert" was and how expertise was developed. It turns out that an "expert" can be anyone who knows more than the general public about a specific topic. The classic example of "expert" may be Marisa Tomei in the movie *My Cousin Vinny*. (If you have not seen the movie, it is worth the time and effort to see it.) For those of you who haven't seen it, Tomei plays Vinny's girl-friend. But she grew up working on cars in the family garage and knows an enormous amount about them—as it turns out, she knows more about cars than the government's expert. So, she becomes an "expert" for the case, and her testimony saves the day. Corny, I know. But still—accurate in terms of how to become an expert.

With my background vocation in the martial arts, I easily qualified as an expert martial artist. After all, I had earned a sixth degree black belt, two fifth degree black belts, and black belts in other martial arts too. And since I had been consulting pro bono on personal and professional security issues for over ten years for lawyers (and had taught several law practice management CLEs on the subject), I was qualified as an expert on that subject too. Now all I had to do was let people know.

## Once You Have a Plan, Implement It

Once I realized what I wanted to do with my spare time, I started to write and network and talk about it. It was actually kind of easy, as all I was doing was telling everyone I knew what I wanted to do once I retired. This went on for about four years; I wrote and published in popular magazines about 4th Amendment and use of force issues. (Fortunately for me, for the past two years there have been many issues to be discussed.) I must have written four or five articles a year on these issues. Not only did I publish these

articles, but I put them up on all my websites, including www
.karatelaw.com, the Martial Arts Law Center's website. They got
a lot of traction there.

In addition, just like any other lawyer, I networked (and am
still networking) like crazy. I speak at retired lawyers' groups, and
I talk to young people at the gym, at my motorcycle club, everywhere. Somebody, always, has questions and wants me to talk to
them and their friends. It's fun and it's a public service. People
need to know their rights.

# Lessons Learned (or Advice That's Worth Only What You Paid for It)

So what advice can I offer a lawyer who is beginning to think about
retirement? Make a plan. Look at what you enjoyed before you
dedicated yourself to the law. Look at those things you did in the
few hours you could spare from being a lawyer and ask yourself
if you want to do more of them. Then list them. Decide if they
could be a future for you—one that will fill your heart, mind, and
soul with joy and contentment. Check your bucket list—or make
one. Figure out what you have to do to achieve your bucket list.

Once you have looked back and forward and have some idea of
where you want to end up, make a plan. How will you get there?
Will you be physically able to do the things you want to do? If
not, make a plan to get ready physically. Ditto mentally. Make
your plan realistic and have intermediate steps so you can check
progress. Do the same thing with your finances. When I described
what I did, I looked at life expectancy, lifestyle, and druthers. You
should do that too.

One last thing: being retired is a career in itself. Don't neglect it.

# 3

## You've Got Options, Lots and Lots and Lots of Options!

*by Jeffrey Allen*

Over time, a lawyer's capacity to practice law improves with experience compared to when the lawyer first started out and then tends to deteriorate in many respects as the lawyer ages. Some of the changes may relate to health and the fact that older lawyers may lack the physical energy required to practice law full-time (especially if they are litigators). To some extent, they compensate for that with offsetting experience. At some point, changes due to age, illness, or medications may impact the lawyer's intellectual capacity as well. Sometimes (often before mental or physical limitations impair the ability to practice), a lawyer simply does not want to continue practicing law. Some recognize that they have reached the point where they cannot (or should not) continue practicing law and are clever enough to stop practicing at that point. Others miss that point and continue practicing, potentially causing serious problems for themselves and their clients.

Choosing to no longer practice or to reduce the time devoted to the practice while you still have the ability to practice at the highest levels is one thing. Knowing whether and when to stop practicing is another issue, and an important one that you should not overlook. Over the years, I have found it very sad to listen to comments made about some very senior lawyers whose actual practices outlived their ability to practice well but did not let that stop them from remaining in practice. Most of us do not want to continue practicing at the expense of our reputations and the quality of our representation of our clients. None of us should want to do that. We want to stop while we still have a good reputation. Whether that means you stop in your late 50s, early 60s, or late 80s will vary depending upon how well you age and how much interest you have in continuing your practice. One thing is absolute: there will come a time when each of us will stop practicing law completely. The question for each of us will be whether we stop practicing before we die or because we died.

Some lawyers have chosen to continue practicing beyond their prime years as they fear no longer being practicing lawyers. Most of us see ourselves as lawyers, and it is a part of our definition of who and what we are. When a lawyer stops practicing, the lawyer remains a lawyer, but because he or she no longer works as a lawyer, self-image sometimes suffers, often causing various symptoms of depression. One of the most critical issues of retirement is making sure that after we retire we remain active to reduce the likelihood of depression. After all, many of us have practiced law for a very long time, longer than any other activity or status we've ever been known by, and stopping the active practice of law becomes a daunting challenge to face.

Both during the time we actively practice and afterward, as a general rule, most of us will find that we enjoy our lives more if we have some particularly interesting, useful, or productive component that makes us want to get up in the morning. That component can come from your practice, but as you remove yourself from the practice, you need to find another source. Potential alternate sources include interacting with your family, a job, a hobby, volunteer work, or a combination of those elements (and others that I intend to include by broadly defining "hobby").

This chapter will focus on some of the opportunities available to you as an experienced lawyer who has reached the point where you choose to stop practicing or to, at least, significantly reduce the time you devote to the practice of law and seek to fill the free time that creates with interesting and/or productive endeavors.

Hypothetically speaking, let's say you have a license to practice law and have actively practiced for a while, but due to whatever reason(s) you have started thinking that you would like to do something else with the rest of your life (or at least part of it). You may or may not have reached the point of wanting to completely retire from the practice of law. You may or may not have reached the point of wanting to reduce the amount of time and effort you devote to the practice of law in order to enable you to do other things. But, you see that handwriting on the wall. Sound familiar? If not, and you have practiced for more than 30 years, you belong to what I believe to constitute the minority of experienced lawyers.

I do not have statistical information that I can cite to you about lawyer burnout. It is a term we hear all too frequently these days. I cannot refer you to a formal survey. I can tell you that most of the experienced (25+ years of practice) lawyers that I have talked to (and that's a lot of lawyers) have expressed interest in getting out of the practice entirely or at least in part. Some do not reach that point until later, but it seems that most of us do eventually. I know I reached it after a bit more than 40 years of practice. As a result, at that point, I started to slow my practice down, impose more limits on the type of cases I would take, reduce the billable and total hours I expected from myself, and free up more time to do other things.

Over the course of the next five years, I continued that process until I finally closed my office and started practicing on a relatively limited part-time basis using my house as my primary work location and arranging to meet with clients at a shared office facility downtown. I never planned on becoming one of those retirees who sat around watching the dust collect on the windowsill. I like the idea of keeping busy and have arranged my life to enable me to do that. I still work part-time (about 10–15 hours per week). My wife and I travel much more for pleasure, and we spend as much time as our children will let us with our grandchildren. We have also adopted a couple of furry kids (a Labrador retriever and a Welsh corgi) that I spend a fair amount of time training. But that was not enough for me. I wanted to do more, so I looked at the things I did before I closed my office and picked some that I wanted to devote more time to doing and continued to do them to keep my brain engaged and my body reasonably active.

In many ways, the person I was before I closed my office made the transition easier for me. I have always considered myself a "renaissance person" with interests in many things. As a result, I always kept several irons in the fire. Throughout most of my career, in addition to practicing law, I did work as an arbitrator and as a mediator; I taught at one of the local universities; I presented at a lot of CLE courses; I wrote countless articles; I became involved in youth and adult soccer as a coach, referee, and administrator; I did a lot of community service work; and I actively participated in the activities of the local, state, and national bar associations. I also had the opportunity to run many different types of businesses as a court-appointed receiver, giving me a better perspective on the business world than I might otherwise have had.

When I decided to slow down, I stopped teaching at the university, and I have cut back the number of CLE courses I accept. I have continued to write articles for several law-related publications and have coauthored five books in the last five years. Although I no longer coach or referee soccer, I have continued my involvement as an administrator at fairly high levels (I currently serve as Chairman of the Board of the U.S. Futsal Federation [indoor soccer]). I also retain involvement in the training and evaluation of futsal referees. While I have cut back on some of my community service and bar association work, I continue to maintain active involvement in both areas. I continue to take cases as a mediator and arbitrator and have kept a reduced number of clients and cases so that I can bill about 15 hours a week. As a result, I have kept myself pretty busy since I closed the doors to my brick-and-mortar office. (Note: It really was a brick-and-mortar office as I rented a portion of the 14th floor of a 15-story yellow-brick building for many years.)

For me, converting from full-time lawyer to part-time/semiretired lawyer did not pose significant issues in finding things to keep myself busy because of all the things in which I involved myself over the years. In all honesty, I think that I lasted in the full-time practice of law as long as I did due, in part, to my other activities. I think that they helped prevent my burnout as a lawyer.

For those of you who have focused so intently and exclusively on the practice of law that you did not develop a lot of outside interests, the prospect of selecting what you will do for the next part of your life may seem more challenging. It does not need to be, however. The simple fact is that the skills you learned as a lawyer can make it very easy for you to do a variety of other things besides practice law. In fact, a great number of law school graduates do not actively practice, and some never go into practice. Instead, they have found a variety of positions in many different businesses. For example, many law school graduates have gone into teaching (not just in law school, but also in various areas of graduate and undergraduate education—business, political science, English, speech, and history, for example). I even know of one lawyer who went back to school to get a teaching credential so she could teach high school after she retired from practicing in her early 50s.

No rule (written or unwritten) requires that you undertake an activity that your legal training and experience prepared you to do. It may well be that you have an interest in a completely unrelated field. Perhaps you enjoy beer and want to get into brewing craft beer or making wine or hard liquor. Perhaps you always wanted to have a restaurant (maybe you get a franchise and run a Jack in the Box, Starbucks, etc.). Maybe you partner with a trained chef and open up the next Michelin-starred restaurant. Maybe you have developed an interest in meditation or physical exercise and end up training people to do those things. I know some retired lawyers who devote their time to the production of art (painting, drawing, photography, composing or playing music, etc.). Some choose to go back to school either to acquire another degree they would like to have or, more often, just to take classes about topics that interest them and give them the opportunity to interact socially and intellectually with others. Another possibility is to organize trips for compensation, sometimes by going on the trip expense-free.

While running different types of businesses requires fine-tuning skill sets and may require specific skills that you will need to acquire by training, practice, or employment, the simple fact that you know how to run a business (a law office) will help you to run other types of businesses. In fact, lawyers who have moved into all of the areas discussed above and many, many more, sometimes starting while they still practiced law and sometimes after leaving the practice, have found success.

The real point here is that nothing about your legal training or experience limits you or your choices, and many things in that training and experience can translate into advantages in other areas. The real question will likely prove to be where in the economic scale you fall as an experienced or retiring lawyer. Do you fit into the class of (1) those who have accumulated enough wealth that they simply want to keep busy and productive but have no need to augment their income; (2) those who do not really need to work to support their retirement but who would enjoy having some additional cash to spend during their retirement; or (3) those who must work to survive during their senior years, must supplement resources available for retirement, and may never get to fully retire? This becomes important to your analysis, as if you fall into one of the first two categories, the amount you earn (if any) from the new activities has far less significance than if you fall into the third classification.

I make the point about earnings needs as, unless you have a reasonable amount of good luck (or hidden talent), you will not likely earn as much doing whatever you focus upon as you did (or can) continuing to practice law. Accordingly, if you fall into the second category, you might consider continuing to practice law (at least part-time); that practice may prove even more important if you fall into the third classification. No matter which category you end up in, the best recommendation I can offer you is to follow your passions. If you find that you have a particular interest in doing something, find a way to work it into your life. For example, if you want to become involved in the restaurant industry but don't want to work full-time at it, you might consider investing in an existing business or (riskier) a startup. You could even consider working part-time in someone else's establishment, whether a fine dining establishment or the local Starbucks.

If you love dogs and want to work with them, you could set yourself up as a dog trainer (if you have those skills or sufficient resources to hire those that do to get your business started) or even a dog walker (which still requires some handling skills if you will walk more than one or two dogs at a time). Alternatively, you could become involved in doggy daycare or the dog-boarding industry. My wife and I have found a location that our dogs love and we think takes excellent care of them. When we travel, we usually do not bring our dogs with us, and we leave them at this venue (which we refer to as the "dog spa"). We have had nice hotel rooms for not much more than what we pay to board the two dogs at the spa. While I have not seen a profit and loss statement for the facility, considering that they appear to have about 100 to 125 dogs there whenever we bring our dogs, they have to be bringing in significant revenue from that operation. As their facility is located in a rural area where land costs are not high, and they require you to bring whatever food you want them to feed your dog, they should be clearing a pretty decent sum of money from the operation.

Let's not forget the possibility of finding a community-service activity that you enjoy and devoting time and effort to that. It could be law-related, such as volunteering to work with an organization to provide legal advice to those who cannot afford to hire a lawyer, or non-law-related, such as getting involved in mentoring young people, working with programs like Meals on Wheels, fundraising for social or political causes . . . the list goes on and on and on and on. Think of Jimmy Carter, who, although he did not practice law and never was a lawyer, did serve a term as president of the United States. He spent a good part of his retirement volunteering to help build houses to aid those who needed shelter.

If you want to continue to practice law but do not want to continue to run your own practice, consider working on a contract basis for other lawyers. That offers you a low-overhead, low-risk way of remaining actively involved in the law without creating excessive demands on your time. You can choose how much work to accept. You can (within certain limits based on the time demands of the assignment you accept) control when and where you perform the work.

Please note that I do not intend the suggestions in this chapter as a laundry list of things you can do that in any way limits the choices available to you. In reality (and within reason), those choices abound and are almost limitless.

From my perspective, lawyers as a group are pretty bright and fairly versatile individuals. They have analytical minds, capable of helping them move into a variety of fields or activities. The key is to find something that you really enjoy doing that will satisfy your urge to contribute to society and, if necessary, provide you with an additional income source to make your retirement (or semi-retirement) work. I cannot speak for every lawyer (and I know that some diehards will disagree with me), but I find the idea of working full-time until I drop dead at my desk unsettling to say the least. (I do know some lawyers who consider that the best way to go.) It is not a fate I wish for myself or anyone else. Use the last part of your life to do something you feel passionate about. Find something that truly fulfills you to replace the practice of law (which, hopefully, fulfilled you for many years). It really makes no difference what you choose. There is no universally right answer that works for all of us and, in fact, probably not just one answer that works for any of us. Whatever you choose, if it fulfills your needs, it works for you. There is no better test.

# 4

A Nontraditional
Law Firm Provides
a Roadmap for Your
Transition to Retirement

*by David J. Leffler*

Culhane Meadows PLLC is a law firm that was set up from the start to break from the traditional law firm structure. Partners all have large law firm backgrounds, but that's where the commonality ends. I joined this firm in February 2017.

The firm is what is called a "cloud-based" law firm. While there are office locations in all of the seven cities in which it has a practice, the lawyers in those cities do not regularly go to those offices. Instead, they practice out of their homes or separately established offices. This permits the firm to save a considerable amount on real-estate overhead and also permits a generous split of fee income: 80% to the partner working on clients that he or she has originated, with the other 20% going to the firm. Billing rates can also be set at much more reasonable levels than at a big firm.

The firm's partners have a more flexible lifestyle due to the technology employed in the firm's operations and the absence of a minimum billable hours requirement. Most of the partners still put in plenty of time, but they do so in the manner and locations that they choose.

# The Empty Nester

Angela Washelesky, a partner in the firm's Chicago office who practices trademark law, is an empty nester, and when she and her husband wanted to escape the Chicago winters, they opted this year to relocate to Charleston, South Carolina, for six weeks. Fortunately, they both had jobs that afforded them the flexibility of working remotely.

Angela could work remotely because of the technology that the firm uses. Documents can be accessed remotely and securely through Worldox, which is a document-management program that keeps client documents safe, readily accessible, searchable, and indexed for all partners at the firm to use and securely access 24/7 from any location. Whether Angela opens her laptop in Chicago or Charleston, the same documents are there for her to access.

While each partner can arrange for support personnel, some of the costs of which can be billed to a client, there are not armies of staff at your beck and call at Culhane Meadows as there are at the big firms. For some partners technology does not eliminate the need for support personnel, but it makes things much easier. The firm's online billing program, Bill4Time, is simple to operate and has some special features to ease the burden of the firm's partners as they enter their time and deal with billing. For example, there are useful reports that can be generated at a click of a button.

One of Angela's favorite Bill4Time features is how easy it makes it to respond to a client's request for a billing history. The old-school way of doing this could take hours, going through old bills and sending the right ones in the right format to the client. With Bill4Time, you just send a link to the client, which takes the client directly into his or her Bill4Time records. The client can then search and review the billing records for as long as necessary.

The freedom of not having to go to an office every day permits Angela to indulge in certain routines. Every workday, whatever the weather, she takes a long walk with one of her younger dogs to the local Starbucks. It gives her time to clear her head and return refreshed to her home office.

Angela's practice does not require her to meet clients very often, but when necessary, a coffee shop or restaurant will often do. The landscape of the practicing lawyer is rapidly changing, and while ten years ago a client might have looked askance at a lawyer without a downtown law office, today a lawyer without a fancy office more often is acknowledged as part of a growing trend.

The thing that Angela likes best about Culhane Meadows is that her working from home does not make her a stepchild; rather, her lifestyle is the norm in the firm. So, while technology enables this lifestyle, the firm's culture supports it.

# Founder's Solution

Kelly Culhane, a founding partner of the firm who is based in Dallas, took a traditional path after graduating from law school of working for a large, international law firm. Several years later, when she was having her first child, she made the decision to leave the practice of law to be home for her children.

When her youngest child was in elementary school, Kelly formed Culhane Meadows with her other founding partners, which permitted her to practice law and still have the depth of involvement that she wanted with raising her children.

Though sometimes there are work-related conflicts that are unavoidable with a sophisticated client base, she is still able to be with her children when they get home from school and attend field trips, sporting events, and other activities. She now has a child playing select soccer traveling out of state for games, and her work is rarely interrupted because her law practice is completely mobile.

One of Kelly's favorite features of the firm's technology is Skype for Business, which permits her to have text or video chats with any partner in the firm. Kelly uses the texting when on a call with a partner and a group of other parties and an offline discussion is needed. The video conference feature is also valuable because after that phone call (or at any other time), Kelly can get on a video chat with the partner to do a post-call analysis, which can be helpful in picking up facial clues and other mannerisms that would simply be missed in a phone call.

Kelly also likes Worldox, the firm's document storage product. This past year Kelly visited the Dominican Republic, Vietnam, South Korea, Japan, the United Kingdom, and Ireland, and yet Kelly remained in close touch with her clients and was able to close more than a handful of deals, which she could not have done without the sophisticated document access features provided by Worldox.

Finally, the firm's culture and technology permit Kelly to spend significant time working to support her favorite charity, the National Center for Missing and Exploited Children. There are times when she needs to be in Austin for a board meeting or fundraising events, and she can do so because her office travels with her.

# World Traveler

Paula Jill Krasny is a partner in the firm's Chicago office and in recent years has traveled to India, Denmark, France, and South Africa. She also became a 200-hour-level certified yoga instructor and has been studying improv at the renowned Second City and iO theaters in Chicago. None of this prevented her from having a great year as a partner at the firm in 2017 and continuing to do well in 2018.

Paula remembers being in Cape Town when a client was evaluating modifying its brand and changing its corporate name. She needed to access documents to be able to strategize with the client and put a team in place for work potentially coming to the firm before she returned to the United States. The cloud-based Worldox document management software greatly assisted. She also appreciates the firm's SecuriSync file sharing portal, which permits her to collaborate on and share documents securely with clients and fellow partners.

Paula believes that lawyers should not be intimidated by technology. They should try to embrace it to efficiently deliver high-quality work for their clients. Don't get stuck in yesterday's technology; learn to adapt to today's technology. Her advice is to get comfortable getting out of your comfort zone because change is the only constant in today's world.

# Young Family

Richard, a Dallas partner, has young children under the age of ten. Family commitments typically require a work "hard stop" at 5:00 p.m.

His arrangement permits him to occasionally have lunch with his children at school, which is right up the street, and he is there for emergencies. And he loves the zero commute time.

A home office setup with young children requires that the children respect their parent's office space. Richard has a separate office space and a routine that his children have learned to respect to avoid any outbursts.

Lawyers on their way to retirement do not typically have to worry about young children, but there is the dog barking in the background that might make your setup sound less than professional. Consider this when planning your office setup. If you are in the midst of choosing a dog, stay away from yappy dogs such as terriers.

Richard notes that Culhane Meadows could not exist without today's technology. He remembers when he had to be in the office to pick up a fax from a client or opposing counsel. The world of emails and PDF attachments has replaced that. Even if a fax does have to be sent, as certain governmental offices still require, it all can be handled online. Just remember to hold on to your scanner if you are starting with a paper document.

Richard is a business bankruptcy lawyer. He explained to me that a normal litigation has maybe 20 to 30 pleadings but that a bankruptcy proceeding has between 2,000 and 3,000 pleadings. Not surprisingly, bankruptcy courts were the first courts to adopt modern technology. Paper filings were replaced with electronic filings of PDF documents, available to all participants in the proceeding. If there is a document that for some reason Richard needs to print and mail out, there are services that will do this for him, eliminating the need for a support staff to get this done. Software now automatically downloads and stores all of the pleadings at minimal cost without hands-on intervention of secretaries, paralegals, or other staff.

All of this works nicely with the firm's technology infrastructure. SecuriSync, Adobe Acrobat, and Bill4Time keep everything electronic and in the cloud, making for seamless connections with the courts.

Richard notes that a Google search that can often turn up valuable information at no charge might have previously taken hours of research in a law library. However, the overlay of an experienced lawyer's analysis is often needed to filter through what is valuable and what is not.

Richard typically answers his own phone, which eliminates the need for a receptionist. If he misses a call, his phone carrier transmits a text transcript of any message left by the caller.

Richard sees all of these tools as freeing lawyers to do what they do best, advise clients on overall strategy and approaches, which is the most valuable time that a lawyer provides to his or her client. They also permit some scaling down of time and the resulting bill on a smaller matter.

# My Story

I am a business lawyer based in New York City, and I travel locally on a regular basis but still maintain a seamless law practice because of the tools mentioned here. I also use Call Ruby, a service located in Oregon, whose staff answers my office phone and screens the call by calling my cellphone to see if I want to take the call. I either accept, and the call is put through to my cellphone, or a message is taken. Since calls are put through to my cellphone, I could be almost anywhere and still be reachable.

I even can do this when out of the country by working with a cellphone that operates through Wi-Fi. The service calls my U.S. cellphone number, and I answer my cellphone using a Wi-Fi connection. Last year I closed a deal for a client when I was in Mexico, made possible, in part, by this piece of phone technology.

Clients assume that I am in my New York City home office when I am often elsewhere. But it doesn't matter where I am because the work is still getting done, promptly and professionally.

I have several options when it comes to meeting clients. If the matter is not confidential, I can meet them at their office, which they appreciate. If the matter requires more privacy, then I can meet them in one of the conference rooms that my bar association has in midtown Manhattan. Sometimes meeting for lunch or at a coffee shop is appropriate as well. Finally, there are companies that are in the business of renting out offices and conference rooms, some of which are quite luxurious; that can be an option as well.

# Your Turn

Technology has transformed our lives in many ways. From smartphones that provide you the world's knowledge in the palm of your hand to having conversations with that phone and home appliances to get that information without touching a keypad, we've really stepped into the future big time.

That same technology permits you to practice law wherever you happen to be with only a laptop computer or even just a smartphone. Everything you need is there—research tools, document drafting tools, and communication tools. Plus, technology permits you to make calls home from anywhere in the world for little or no money.

If someone had intentionally designed a system for downsizing your law practice as you eased into retirement, they could not have done a better job. Lawyers looking to wind down their practice to eventual retirement need flexibility, because they are often looking to spend more time traveling or with children and grandchildren. Lawyers on the retirement track want to do their lawyering from wherever they are, and the good news is that now you can.

# 5

## Scaling Back a Practice to Part-Time, Winding Down, and Changing Practice Specialties and Practice Styles

*by Robin Page West*

As we approach the fourth or so decade of law practice, the idea of scaling back, pivoting to a new substantive area, or changing our practice setting seems to pop up. It's tempting to make a change in order to avoid something unpleasant. But it's important to factor in what you are yearning for. No one wants to take pains to get rid of one problem only to walk right into a new one. Making changes could mean lower overhead expenses, a shorter time frame for getting paid, more interesting subject matter, a different type of client, and so on. Once the goal is identified, it's easier to achieve.

I have difficulty mustering the confidence to make changes. I tend to stick with whatever's working until things get to the point that I must take action. It seems the better course would be to figure out the right move and do it slowly and methodically. But for much of my career, it didn't happen that way. I made a few pivots, not always totally the way I would have planned, but they still worked out fine.

Whether you're making change on your own terms or reacting to events beyond your control, it's daunting to think about pivoting. Analysis paralysis sets in, and we obsess about making a mistake or failing. We ask ourselves, if I change my practice, how will I get clients, will my current clients stay with me, where will I get the administrative support I need, how will I learn what I need to know in order to move into a different area, and on and on.

In hindsight, I say worry less and trust yourself to be resilient and resourceful.

For example, haven't you already developed, many times over, new areas of expertise? What about when you first started out? My first job as an associate was with the national coordinating counsel for a major chemical company, working on its insulation fire litigation. I was to take and defend depositions in cases resulting from fires involving the product that were venued from Alaska to the U.S. Virgin Islands. I was also tasked with organizing all the information gleaned in the depositions for ready retrieval at a later date. I threw myself into the job and developed some sophisticated systems and best practices for deposition-taking and cataloging in products liability cases. It was challenging and interesting, but after a few years, I got tired of the narrow focus. Another firm interviewed me and immediately offered a position, saying I would be working on a large number of diverse litigation matters. For a short time, this was true, until one day they landed an enormous contract to defend some large manufacturers and I was tapped to—wait for it—take and defend depositions involving one particular product—asbestos. Drat! Pigeonholed again!

However unintentionally, I had developed an expertise in products liability discovery phase litigation that was valuable and sought after. At the time, I was oblivious to the ease with which I had developed this expertise or even to the fact that it set me apart from other lawyers. We all have expertise developed over the years that we may take for granted. Take a moment and reflect on all the areas in which you've developed competency. How did you do it? Can you repeat the scenario with a new area? If you are doubtful, why? Could you be underestimating your capacity for developing new expertise?

I was totally stumped about how to escape the deposition drudgery that seemed to be dogging me. If I went to yet another firm, would the same thing happen again? What about government or corporate work? As I ruminated over this, my personal life took center stage. I got married and became pregnant. Initially this seemed like a big problem, career-wise, given that I planned to make the new baby first priority. What I needed was an exquisitely flexible practice that would let me call all the shots. The options I was considering before went right out the window. The only answer was to start my own firm. Being young, optimistic, and a little bit desperate, I went ahead and did it. Not because I thought it was the best way to a successful legal career (which it ultimately proved to be), but rather because it was the only way I could figure out at the time (over 30 years ago) to be present as a mother and keep my legal career going. I had to juggle a lot, but I managed. A second child arrived, and my solo practice flourished. The pivot worked.

I did not so much choose solo practice as I accepted it and made it work because it was the only viable alternative. I didn't have to analyze my chances of success and compare them to other types of practice because there was nothing to compare it to. My focus was not on whether it would work but rather on how to make it work. Had the choice not been made for me by circumstances, I doubt I would have been confident enough to go out on my own. What about you? Have circumstances ever prompted you to make a change you'd never considered before? Did you rise to the occasion and do the necessary to make it work? Shifting our perspective from "what will happen if I do this?" to "how can I make this work?" allows our brains to focus not on the unknown but the known. When we focus on the known, it's less frightening, and actually empowering, to make changes.

After about five years of solo practice doing primarily plaintiff's contingent fee litigation without regard to subject area, I overheard a cocktail party conversation about the False Claims Act, which at the time was a little-used statute that allows someone with knowledge of fraud on the government to file a lawsuit on behalf of the government to recover the funds and share in the recovery. This seemed like a fascinating area of practice. I made a mental note and may have even wondered how to break into such a specialized field, one that I hadn't even heard of before. But I didn't do anything about it. Some time later, though, a friend referred a client who had one of these cases. She had been looking for a lawyer with this expertise but hadn't found anyone. It was time for me to study up on the law and seek co-counsel with a track record. I approached several of the leading firms in this area and got nowhere but eventually formed a co-counsel relationship with one of the other lawyers in that cocktail party conversation, and we moved forward with the case. Eventually it settled and was the fourth-largest such recovery nationwide that year. Afterward, my client and I received press coverage and were invited to meet President Clinton and Vice President Gore. I was asked to give some talks at bar association meetings. This resulted in enough new cases that from then on it became my primary practice area. I kept up my speaking engagements and soon realized that my notes from the speeches were enough to make a book. Once the book was published, it established me as somewhat of an expert in the field.

Here again, this was not something I selected as the best practice area for me. It was the synergy of that cocktail party chitchat and the referral of a client—two things that happened, seemingly randomly—that allowed me to enter a niche practice area with very little competition and lots of opportunity. There is apparently no limit to the creativity on display when vendors are trying every way they can think of to defraud the government. Again, I have to believe that if my friend had not referred that client, whom I really wanted to help because my friend referred her, I would never have taken the plunge into such a specialized area of practice. I would not have had the confidence. But when pushed, I rose to the occasion.

I continued to practice as a solo in this field. The lawsuits are filed under seal, and my clients are not permitted to divulge the suit's existence. This made me their only sounding board. Often their case was the most important thing going on in their lives. They needed to talk to someone about it, and I felt a great responsibility to them. Every moment of my time in the office was spent on client work or evaluating potential new cases. I enjoyed my practice; I loved, respected, and admired my clients; and I could not imagine any other substantive area that could be more interesting or rewarding. And yet I was becoming depleted. What I needed was some office collegiality, some water cooler chitchat, to break up the day and give me the opportunity to think about something else now and then.

Around this time, a lawyer I knew who was about 25 years my senior was making a pivot of his own, away from litigation. He sought to continue representing his corporate and estate clients but wanted someone else to go to court for him on routine hearings and calendar calls. He had two secretaries and an associate who didn't do litigation. I liked them. The prospect of doing some low-stakes courtroom work in a different practice area, and the idea of having other people to talk to at the office, was appealing. I wasn't interested in sharing revenue from my own cases, and neither was he. So we formed a firm where we shared expenses but kept our practices and earnings separate. He was the primary user of the associate, clerical, and administrative staff, while I managed with only a modicum of staff support through judicious use of technology tools and reliance on the rapid typing skills I had honed in journalism school.

This arrangement worked well for over ten years. A few lawyers came and went, as did support staff, but there was a core of us who stuck together. The first inkling that things were coming to an end was when he floated the idea that our overhead expense-sharing agreement be modified to increase my share of the expenses. Although this didn't go over well with me, I didn't want to pack up my toys and leave. I liked my coworkers and the cozy, collegial firm that had developed over the years. The firm was family to me, and I wanted to remain a part of it. I made a counter-proposal. How about if I vacate the corner office and my parking spot? Everything else would continue as before: I would have the same minimal administrative support, access to the conference room, photocopier, all IT systems, malpractice insurance, etc. I would continue as an owner with my name on the door. Nothing would change other than I would telecommute. In exchange, my share of the expenses would be reduced, and he could either use or sublet my former office. He agreed.

I ported my direct-dial office landline to a cellphone so my clients could use the same number as always to reach me. From that point on, I made my phone calls and did my written work from home, going to the office mainly to pick up mail and for client meetings, staff meetings, and office parties. Even though I still saw my coworkers fairly regularly, it was only in short bursts of time, so the bonds that formed when we were together every weekday from nine to six started to loosen. I didn't learn as much about their personal lives, and I no longer served as mediator in various and sundry office dramas. I didn't get to hear as many war stories. To be sure, I missed this, but at the same time, now I had a lot more time to focus on other things.

One of them was finances. I spent hours poring over my own money matters to discern trends and map out a plan for financial independence. I learned that because the type of cases I handled took many years to show a positive cash flow, it made more sense to stop taking new cases and focus on concluding the ones already in process than to take on new cases and commit to expenses that might not be recouped for five or even ten more years, if ever. Sometimes when you are completely busy with day-to-day details, planning for long-term goals gets pushed to the side, and this lack of clarity can make things seem worse than they really are. I double-checked my findings with a few personal financial advisors and accountants and made the decision to start tapering down my practice immediately.

Evaluating new client matters was a large part of my daily routine. In fact, it may have consumed more time than the actual representation of current clients. Once I eliminated that activity, I had a great deal of newfound freedom. I surprised myself, because instead of looking for some other type of work to do that would have generated fees more regularly, I started filling that time with fun and leisure activities and began to realize that despite how much I loved my law practice, I might actually be ready to move on. Even so, I had trouble reconciling myself to the concept of squandering my earning power. I was having difficulty figuring out which way to go.

Meanwhile, my partner fell ill and stopped coming to the office. Although he told us he would be returning soon, we decided to assess his work in progress to make sure all current clients were properly represented. Soon after we began, he passed away.

Here is another pivot point that I most certainly did not choose. While I was ruminating over whether to close my own practice, events transpired that pushed me, the sole surviving shareholder, into closing his. The first step was to meet with all firm employees to create a roadmap and a timeline for closing.

We searched for law firm closing checklists and found several to guide us. Then we examined the firm's financial situation to determine how long we could support salaries and expenses without the partner's billings. This gave us a general idea of how much time we had either to sell or to close the practice. We then set about working down the items on the checklists, which included, but were not limited to, notifying clients; assessing all active matters; arranging for representation for all clients and transferring their files; arranging for return of any funds held in escrow; creating and implementing a document retention/storage/destruction policy; indexing and storing all retained files and data; negotiating buyouts of the lease, equipment rentals, and contracts; closing bank accounts; and finding new jobs for the remaining employees.

This was a months-long process during which we met regularly, updated each other on our progress, read old files, and reminisced about events gone by. It was bittersweet. We remembered those times fondly but knew without doubt that we were all ready for a new beginning. We wouldn't have taken this path if we had the choice, but we were going to make the best of it.

# Part II

# When the Decision Is Not the Lawyer's Own

The transition from actively practicing law to a second act isn't always the lawyer's own decision to make, and often it doesn't come at the most convenient time. Just like the rest of the population, lawyers age. Maturity, wisdom, and a seasoned view on life and the practice of law can give way to unsettling circumstances and outcomes.

**Chapter 6**

How Cognitive Decline Affects Lawyers
*Scott R. Mote*

**Chapter 7**

Addressing Ethical Issues Facing the Aging Lawyer
*Ted A. Waggoner*

**Chapter 8**

Strategies for Dealing with the Lawyer Who Refuses
to Discuss Retirement
*Ted A. Waggoner*

# 6

# How Cognitive Decline Affects Lawyers

*by Scott R. Mote*

Although the average retirement age in the United States is just 63, almost a quarter of Americans believe they won't retire until age 70 or older.[1] This also holds true for lawyers. Whether a lawyer is working past the average retirement age to beef up his or her 401(k), or the lawyer is not quite ready to call it quits, as the brain ages, the lawyer could suffer from cognitive issues that could be detrimental to clients. Approximately one in ten adults over the age of 65 has some form of mild cognitive impairment (MCI)— problems with memory and/or other thinking abilities that exceed those associated with normal aging.[2]

Over the last few years, Lawyer Assistance Programs (LAPs) have received many referrals regarding elderly lawyers and their diminished capacity to practice law, and these referrals will only continue to increase. According to the U.S. Census Bureau, more than 20% of U.S. residents are projected to be age 65 and over

---

1. Maurie Backman, *Is 70 the New Retirement Age?*, USA TODAY (Sept. 16, 2016), https://www.usatoday.com/story/money/personalfinance/2016/09/16/is-70-the-new -retirement-age/90256526/?showmenu=true.

2. Nicole D. Anderson, *Living with Mild Cognitive Impairment*, PSYCHOLOGY TODAY BLOG (Nov. 30, 2012), https://www.psychologytoday.com/us/blog/living-mild-cognitive -impairment/201211/living-mild-cognitive-impairment.

by 2030.[3] According to the NOBC-APRL-CoLAP Second Joint Committee Report on Aging Lawyers, Final Report-April 2014, more than 50% of lawyers will soon be over 50 years old, if they aren't already.[4] This means that there will be many lawyers who will continue to practice well beyond age 65, which could lead to many issues that come along with age.

Dealing with cognitive decline in the legal profession is challenging. Many lawyers practice beyond the average retirement age, yet their bodies and minds undoubtedly do not function as well as they used to. As lawyers, it is our duty to serve and protect the public and protect the integrity of the law, yet some of us might be causing unintended harm to our clients because of the way our minds and bodies change as we age. Whether we are experiencing health-related issues, cognitive impairment, or both, it is our duty to protect our clients and make sure that we are competent to practice law.

# Medical Implications

Lawyers inevitably will struggle with health issues as they age. For many, the aging process is what will impact the ability to continue to practice law in the same manner to which they have grown accustomed over the years.

Each person is unique, there is no stereotype as to how we age, and not all age-related changes are harmful or negative. Scientists suggest that aging is likely a combination of many factors, including genetics, lifestyle, and disease. Physical changes include:

---

3. Jennifer M. Ortman, Victoria A. Velkoff & Howard Hogan, *An Aging Nation: The Older Population in the United States*, U.S. Census Bureau (May 2014), https://www.census.gov/prod/2014pubs/p25-1140.pdf.

4. NOBC-APRL-CoLAP Second Joint Committee on Aging Lawyers, Final Report (Apr. 2014), https://www.americanbar.org/content/dam/aba/administrative/lawyer_assistance/ls_colap_nobc_aprl_colap_second_joint_committee_aging_lawyers.authcheckdam.pdf.

- Eyesight issues involve loss of peripheral vision and decreased ability to judge depth. There is decreased clarity of colors (for example, pastels and blues).
- Hearing issues involve loss of hearing acuity, especially sounds at the higher end of the spectrum. There is also decreasing ability to distinguish sounds when there is background noise.
- Taste is affected with decreased taste buds and saliva.
- Touch and smell are affected with decreased sensitivity to touch and ability to smell.
- Decreased ability to react to the environment.
- Arteries stiffen with age and fatty deposits build up in the blood vessels over time, eventually causing arteriosclerosis (hardening of the arteries).
- The heart thickens with age. Maximum pumping rate and the body's ability to extract oxygen from the blood both diminish with age.
- Bladder function may be affected, resulting in increased frequency of urination, and kidneys shrink and become less efficient.
- Around age 20, lung tissue begins to lose its elasticity, and rib cage muscles shrink progressively. Maximum breathing capacity diminishes with each decade of life.
- Around age 35, bones start to lose minerals faster than they are replaced.
- The brain gradually loses some of the structures that connect nerve cells, and the function of the cells themselves is diminished. "Senior moments" increase.
- Sexual health is affected by decreased hormone levels, with women going through menopause and men experiencing enlarged prostate.
- Body fat changes. It increases until middle age, stabilizes until later in life, then decreases. The distribution of fat shifts—moving from just beneath the skin to surround deeper organs.

- Muscle mass declines, especially with lack of exercise.
- Skin becomes dry and more wrinkled. It also heals more slowly and nails grow more slowly.
- Metabolism changes, meaning medicines and alcohol are not processed as quickly. Prescription medication requires adjustment.
- Reflexes are slowed while driving, etc.

These changes involve body function and appearance changes, but a main concern for aging practicing lawyers is cognitive impairment. Cognitive impairment occurs when there is a problem with perceiving, thinking, and remembering. Aging, physical illness, mental health issues, and alcohol and drug interactions are all possible causes of cognitive impairment.

# Types of Cognitive Impairment

An example of normal age-related memory loss is when you walk into a room and forget why you went there. Abnormal cognitive decline occurs when you forget important details from recent life events, or you repeat the same question several times. You might have trouble finding words or following simple directions.

In addition to the typical cognitive decline that all people face as they age, dementia, Alzheimer's disease, and delirium are all possible medical issues that can occur in aging lawyers.

## Dementia

Dementia is the development of multiple cognitive deficits manifested by both memory impairment (impaired ability to learn new information or to recall previously learned information) and one or more of the following cognitive disturbances:

- Aphasia (language disturbance)
- Apraxia (impaired ability to carry out motor activities despite intact motor function)

- Agnosia (failure to recognize or identify objects despite intact sensory function)
- Disturbance in executive functioning (i.e., planning, organizing, sequencing, abstracting)

These cognitive deficits cause significant impairment in social or occupational functioning and represent a significant decline from a previous level of functioning.

## Alzheimer's Disease

Alzheimer's disease is a brain disease that causes problems with memory, thinking, and behavior. It is the most common cause of dementia. It is not a normal part of the aging process, and it is not the only cause of memory loss. Alzheimer's disease worsens over time, and there is no cure. The treatments available try to slow progression and lessen the symptoms.

## Delirium

Delirium is a disturbance of consciousness (i.e., reduced clarity of awareness of the environment) with reduced ability to focus, sustain, or shift attention. There is also a change in cognition (such as memory deficits, disorientation, or language disturbance) or the development of a perceptual disturbance that is not better accounted for by a preexisting, established, or evolving dementia.

The disturbance develops over a short period of time (usually hours to days) and tends to fluctuate during the course of the day. Lastly, upon evaluation, this disturbance is caused by the direct physiological consequences of a general medical condition.

## Mental Health Implications

Mental health implications are a large part of the concern with an aging population in general and lawyers in particular. While many aging people go through the later stages of life successfully and embrace their new phase of life, some people experience mental health issues at this time.

Depression is often the most significant and under-diagnosed mental illness. While depression and suicide rates among the elderly are significant, depression is not a normal part of the aging process.

Suicide is more common among older adults than any other age group, accounting for 16% to 25% of the suicides in the United States. However, it is under-recognized and under-treated. Studies have shown that up to 75% of older adults who kill themselves visited a physician within a month before their death. The risk of suicide increases with other illnesses and when the ability to function becomes limited.

# The Effects of Cognitive Impairment on Lawyers and Clients

The following are just two scenarios that aging lawyers may face.

## Bob, the Disorganized and Confused Lawyer

Bob has been practicing for 50-plus years. He's been a competent lawyer, never any front-page cases, but always timely and professional. He served as local bar president 30 years ago. He practiced with the same excellent firm for most of his career, and his former partners have all retired and moved to sunnier climes or passed away. Bob's wife of nearly 50 years died last year, and his children and grandchildren are scattered across the country. Now it's just Bob and his secretary, who has been with him the last 30 years; she's in her early to mid-70s.

For his entire career, Bob has been a well-respected member of the bar and community. The profession has watched him age gracefully and noticed him slowing down the last ten years or so.

He's still dressed impeccably, and his secretary came with him to court today (a first!).

Bob represents a small business owner in a lease dispute with a commercial landlord. The roof leaked, and the case is about water damage to the business's property. Bob settled with his client's insurer and is seeking the rest of his damages from the landlord. It's a bench trial.

Bob gives an unneeded and disorganized opening statement that is full of references to papers that he drops on the floor twice; his client and secretary retrieve and reorganize them for him. He speaks in halting half sentences and looks at the American flag with a blank stare. Defense counsel waives opening statement, and Bob puts his client on the stand. After establishing that his client's name is David Klein and that he owns the business, Bob stops and looks at opposing counsel for what seems like a minute, saying nothing. He then turns to his client and addresses him as Mr. Anderson, who happens to be the landlord's representative sitting with defense counsel. Mr. Klein graciously corrects Bob, who seems oblivious to his mistake, and Bob looks at the judge and says, "Please instruct the witness to answer the question."

## Gene, a Lawyer Who Misses Deadlines and Becomes Irritable When Questioned

Gene is 74 years old and has been a sole practitioner his entire career. His general practice was always steady, with an emphasis on probate matters. He could administer an estate in his sleep.

Gene lost his long-term secretary three years ago and is struggling to operate his practice with part-time help from the local bar association's secretary referral service. Gene's technological skills are challenged by making his cellphone work.

Gene has nine open cases in probate court. Six of them have problems with timely filing—inventories and fiduciary accounts are overdue. He has been cited to appear on all of them and has promised to get things cleaned up. The new due dates have come and gone, and it's time to send citations again. Two clients have called the court, complaining that Gene is not responsive to their requests to get their parents' estates finished.

Gene comes in to open a new estate on Tuesday. The paperwork is incorrect, and the filing is refused. A court employee points out what corrections need to be made. Gene is reminded that he has six other cases in arrears. He promises to get everything done by next Wednesday.

Gene is back in court on Friday afternoon with the new case that was rejected on Tuesday. The initial errors are not corrected, and Gene seems oblivious to his mistakes. He argues with the court employee, reminding her that he was doing this legal work before she was born, and since she's not a lawyer, her opinion is irrelevant.

When reminded that he has six other cases to get cleaned up by next Wednesday, Gene looks surprised and denies knowing anything about them.

Both lawyers in these fictional scenarios are suffering from age-related cognitive decline, which has affected their clients. They do not purposely harm their clients. They may not even understand or be aware that their minds are causing them to make mistakes, miss deadlines, and even become insensitive to others. But you can see how cognitive decline can cause unintended consequences for clients.

When lawyers suffer from cognitive impairment, it can cause serious consequences—not only for the clients, but also for the lawyer.

In 2011, the Iowa Supreme Court Disciplinary Board alleged that an Iowa lawyer violated 17 Iowa Rules of Professional Conduct while working on foreclosure and bankruptcy matters. He previously was publicly reprimanded in 1999 and 2007, and he voluntarily placed his license on inactive status in 2009. The lawyer admitted that he "desperately hung on too long" to his practice, and the court held that illness can be a mitigating factor with respect to discipline. During the time of the violations, the lawyer was suffering from advanced diabetes, high blood pressure, extreme stress, early-onset dementia, tremors, and restless leg syndrome. The lawyer's license was suspended for one year.[5]

In 2011, the Dayton Bar Association charged an Ohio lawyer with multiple violations of the Rules of Professional Conduct for his alleged mishandling and neglect of two probate matters for a client. The lawyer missed court deadlines, failed to appear for court hearings, and failed to keep in contact with his client.

During the Board of Commissioners on Grievances and Discipline hearing, the panel became concerned about the lawyer's cognitive abilities and memory. At that time, the lawyer was 71 years old, and he repeatedly explained that his confusion was the reason he neglected the probate matters. The lawyer was examined by a psychiatrist, who diagnosed him with age-associated cognitive decline, which likely impaired his ability to deliver quality legal services. The court found that this diagnosis was relevant to determining the appropriate sanction.

The board recommended that the lawyer be suspended for two years, with the entire suspension stayed on the conditions that he complete continuing legal education courses as recommended by the panel, serve two years of monitored probation, contact the Ohio Lawyers Assistance Program, undergo an assessment, and enter into a contract with OLAP.[6]

The lawyers in these cases did not intend to harm their clients. The lawyers acknowledged their wrongdoings, demonstrated good character, and cooperated in the disciplinary investigation. Unfortunately, no treatment is available for age-associated cognitive decline and, in these cases, the lawyers' cognitive decline impaired their ability to provide quality legal services.

---

5. Iowa Supreme Court Attorney Disciplinary Board v. Dunahoo, No. 11-0249 (June 24, 2011), *available at* https://caselaw.findlaw.com/ia-supreme-court/1572315.html.

6. Dayton Bar Association v. O'Neal, 134 Ohio St. 3d 361 2012-Ohio-5634, *available at* http://www.supremecourt.ohio.gov/rod/docs/pdf/0/2012/2012-Ohio-5634.pdf.

# Reporting

As lawyers, we have a responsibility to protect the public and maintain the integrity of the legal profession, but what do you do if you witness a lawyer or judge who you think is suffering from age-related cognitive decline? The short answer is to report the person. According to Rule 5.1 of the Model Rules of Professional Conduct, you must make reasonable efforts to ensure that other lawyers conform to the Rules of Professional Conduct. That might sound harsh and easier said than done, but remember that you are trying to help not only the lawyer, but also the clients who might be affected.

The first step is to contact your state LAP. These programs can do an assessment or make a referral for one and help aging lawyers navigate the difficult process of changing how they practice or retiring from the practice of law. Each case will be handled individually and with compassion.

# Create a Positive Environment

Regardless of the issues facing the lawyer, it is essential that those involved with the aging lawyer create a positive environment and good rapport. It is essential to uphold the dignity of the individual. We must respect how much one's self-worth, self-esteem, and self-confidence are all connected to the identity of being a lawyer. This difficult life transition can be made more tolerable if we allow the aging lawyer as much control and input as possible during this process.

# ABA MODEL RULES OF PROFESSIONAL CONDUCT AND COGNITIVE IMPAIRMENT

Tracy L. Kepler, director of the ABA's Center for Professional Responsibility, pointed out several rules that should be considered when dealing with cases of cognitive impairment.

## Rule 1.1—Competence

Cognitive impairment can cause aging lawyers to struggle with this most basic rule: providing competent representation to a client.

## Rules 1.3 and 1.4—Diligence and Communication

Forgetfulness stemming from cognitive impairment can lead to missed deadlines and lack of follow-through in communicating with clients.

## Rule 1.6—Confidentiality of Information

Aging lawyers may unintentionally disclose confidential information by simply not being as careful.

## Rule 1.16—Declining or Terminating Representation

Attorneys must withdraw if a physical or mental condition is impeding their ability to serve clients.

## Rule 5.1—Responsibilities of Partners, Managers, and Supervisory Lawyers

Partners or supervisors must make reasonable efforts to ensure that other lawyers conform to the Rules of Professional Conduct and, in some cases, can be held responsible for another lawyer's violation of the rules.

## Rule 8.3—Reporting Professional Misconduct

Lawyers are required to inform the appropriate professional authority if they know that another lawyer has committed a violation of the Model Rules of Professional Conduct.

# 7

# Addressing Ethical Issues Facing the Aging Lawyer

*by Ted A. Waggoner*

Legal ethics are complex issues, with rules and comments that are necessarily vague but with significant impact and effect. The rules are applied mostly when a client, opponent, or opposing counsel makes a complaint or report to the state supreme court's disciplinary agency (here called Bar Counsel) due to some mistreatment by the lawyer or other violation of the rules as perceived by the complainant. The vagueness comes from a need to cover a variety of possible actions that may have caused a bad outcome for a client, an adverse party, a witness, or the justice system.

## Pushing the Ethical Boundaries

Let's take it as a given that certain ethical violations are going to be treated as disqualifying lawyers from the practice of law. Stealing client funds or other trust fund violations; sexual relations with a client, consensual or not; and lying to the tribunal all will result in significant troubles for lawyers who break the rules, no matter their age or experience.

These offenses are often reported by persons with no skin in the game, such as the bank filing reports on trust fund overdrafts that then lead to an investigation showing theft of funds and other violations, or a judge who reports a counsel's lies, false evidence, and other violations of courtroom ethics.

Other ethical violations are harder to spot since lawyers operate in a variety of settings, from courtroom battles to boardroom negotiations to office consultations. Many legal transactions occur where there is no seemingly neutral referee to throw a flag if an ethical infraction or worse is observed. The more effective potential observers of ethical violations are judges, opposing counsel, jurors, or litigants in a courtroom. In a boardroom, it could be the client, the other party to the negotiations, or that party's counsel who reports, while in the office conferences it is normally clients, those affected by the clients' actions, or office staff who raises the concern.

This is not a suggestion that pushing ethical boundaries is a good idea for lawyers of any age. For years, lawyers have tried to skirt the rules, but the focus here is on those issues that affect aging lawyers and their fellow attorneys, staff, and clients. Some disabilities can be affected by or related to age, but this focus is the aging, not the disability.

It appears to be generally true that as lawyers age, their in-court presence often drops, and their boardroom or office practice increases. Thus, their exposure to the anger of a litigant, an opposing party, their attorney, a witness, or even a disgruntled client drops off. Higher emotional involvement in legal matters makes ethical problems more likely to take place, and staying out of those places limits the exposure to ethical complaints. Litigation is also real-time combat; many decisions must be made in the moment of the hearing.

In court, ethical actions and decisions include evidentiary matters such as whether to submit evidence or object to opponent's evidence; implementing courtroom tactics while dealing with witnesses, counsel, judge, and jurors; strategy management; and maintaining decorum for the parties and system.

This is not to say that transactional lawyers are more ethical than litigators, or that avoiding complaints to Bar Counsel proves that a lawyer is ethical. Reading disciplinary cases is proof that there are problem lawyers across all aspects of the law. It does show that more ethical issues come from the violation of duties in litigation, because the deadlines are stricter and with more serious or immediate consequences.

One other aspect is that aging lawyers often work with long-term clients and as a result get the benefit of the doubt about the ethical nature of a problem that occurs. Long-term clients are often able to resolve issues with the lawyer or firm without the need to involve Bar Counsel. Or they accept part of the blame for knowing that they had hired an aging lawyer with attendant issues. Long-term clients are often the best to have in a time that needs some understanding.

# Identifying and Resolving the Problems

Neglect of files and neglect of clients are among the leading ethical concerns for aging lawyers. Older lawyers are susceptible to the issue of neglect due to distraction or age-related memory illnesses. Problems can be solved or avoided if staff members are attentive enough to help deal with the consequences of age-related memory problems. Regular review of all open files and the use of a two-entry system to confirm that listed "open files" are the actual active files that must be managed is one effective means of avoiding the problem.

Competence is another serious concern. Recent changes to the Comments to Rule 1.1 (see Comment 8 to the Model Rules of Professional Conduct, which has been adopted by several states) are an indication that computerization and the many changes to the legal practice, including word processing, practice management software, e-discovery rule changes, and e-filing of court documents, put a burden on all lawyers. Lawyers are required to shoulder that burden on behalf of their clients.

Aging Baby Boomers started practice in a day of printed decennial digests and Shepard's Citation. The use of computers for legal research was in its infancy. Gen X and younger lawyers generally are more adept at adapting to the computerization of the legal world. The result is that aging lawyers are more likely to fall into incompetence due to a failure to maintain full computerization skills.

Preparation for upcoming matters is also a critical issue, since different matters require different lead time for preparation. Drafting documents, avoiding statutes of limitation, and witness preparation are part of the arsenal of litigators of all kinds of cases, from small claims to complex litigation. The smaller the team of lawyers, the more important it is for the lead counsel to stay on top of preparation. Again, staff members who are knowledgeable about litigation may help avoid a breach of ethics.

At some point the complex issues involved in handling litigation, including drafting pleadings, responding to discovery, and negotiating cases, become nondelegable to staff. Staff does not owe the client the fiduciary duty of competence. Competence is the duty of the lawyer, and when the lawyer loses the ability to perform, ethical problems arise.

The competence issue may be the undoing of many aging lawyers. Staying on top of changes in statutes, case law, and now computer skills may simply overwhelm many lawyers or subject them to grievances.

In the work I have done with aging lawyers, I find that some lawyers are slow to self-identify the existence of practice problems, and so it is important that those they work with have the strength to report problems and concerns to the lawyer or the lawyer's partners or associates. Lack of attention to details, forgetfulness, loss of skills, or other problems are indications of concerns and triggers to intervene with the aging lawyer.

Partners and staff need to protect themselves professionally by paying attention to signs and signals of problems. See Chapter 8 for means and methods of dealing with the troubled aging lawyer.

# Disciplinary Matters

There is good news and bad news about disciplinary cases involving older lawyers. The good news is that there are not too many cases reported. Occasionally you may find a case that indicates age is a problem, but not often. Neither the *Restatement of the Law Third—The Law Governing Lawyers* nor *The Lawyer's Deskbook on Professional Responsibility* has an index for aging or older attorneys by whatever name.

Discussions with current and retired Bar Counsel indicate that the disciplinary commissions and state supreme courts usually take a gentle approach to lawyers suffering age-related issues (not to be confused with theft of funds or other issues), for which many lawyers are grateful.

The bad news is that the expected resolution is to have the accused lawyer retire their license to practice law in exchange for the resolution of the complaint. If there are damages resulting from the ethical violation, restitution is usually a condition of accepting the retirement. Most states distinguish between resigned licenses and retired licenses, and that distinction helps in getting the disciplinary issue resolved.

The natural outcome for a competence complaint will be retirement, since once a lawyer gets behind the curve on computerization issues, the ability to overcome that problem will be quite difficult. The new comment on competence may lead to more lawyers retiring at younger ages than would have occurred without that rule change.

That may be a good thing.

# 8

## Strategies for Dealing with the Lawyer Who Refuses to Discuss Retirement

*by Ted A. Waggoner*

Let's be blunt—sometimes we have to deal with lawyers who are past their prime, whose skills are significantly weakened: lawyers who need to slow down or retire. Being lawyers, they carry the necessary talents to be generally disagreeable or may simply have a blind spot as to their lost skills. This chapter is designed to help partners, associates, staff, or family members in this usually delicate, sometimes brutal effort to retire the lawyer who won't go easily into retirement.

While some of these strategies may work on lawyers whom you want to get out of a case as opposing counsel, the chapter is designed for firm members dealing with some of those "nonperforming" lawyers whose legal skills have dropped off due to any of several factors. It is focused on lawyers who will not or cannot any longer do the work needed by a professional who is representing clients. They no longer bother to look at statutes or cases; they don't interview clients or cannot recall the content of client interviews or phone calls. Their work gets lost or is not completed; they miss deadlines; their billing receipts drop. In smaller firms, this lawyer is often a founder of the firm.

There are lots of reasons for the problems, but one thing is clear—the lawyer is no longer competent to properly represent clients and needs to stop trying to do so.

There are other reasons partners will have a need to remove their law partners, but this chapter is devoted to the more senior lawyers, often firm founders, or longtime successful lawyers who now need to move on.

# Background Issues

There are background issues that must be identified by the rest of the firm, since no one strategy will fit all older lawyers (I will use "lawyer" for the older lawyer throughout this chapter and "partner" for the younger lawyer or lawyers wanting to move the senior lawyer into retirement):

- Medical Issues—The onset of memory issues is a medical matter. While some medical matters can be overcome, memory issues seriously affect the ability to competently practice law. It is a primary reason for the need for this chapter. As a partner you will not likely have access to medical information on the lawyer, unless the partnership agreement provides HIPAA-approved access to a partner's medical records. If medical issues are the source of the problem, the partner may or may not have an ally in the lawyer's physician due to professional considerations of the physician.
- Hardheadedness—If the lawyer is simply hardheaded and refuses to acknowledge evidence of fading skills, this will be a difficult type of case to address. Hardheaded lawyers usually associate that talent with competence. "If I

can frustrate my partners, just think of how I can succeed against opposing counsel." It does not work that way.

- The What/Who Paradox—Retirement pushes lawyers across the what/who line. It forces a recognition that lawyers are moving from basing their identity on what they do—"I am a lawyer, I handle [insert elevator speech]"—to who they are. "I am a retired lawyer who loves reading, golf, gardening, family, and [insert new passion that has nothing to do with clients or courtrooms]." Losing the "what" identity is tougher if the lawyer has not yet identified the "who" at the core of his or her life.

- Rules of Persuasion Apply Here—Just as you need to use the rules of persuasion to convince a jury of the right results in your client's case, you may need to use the rules of persuasion to advance the concept of retirement or letting go of the practice. A partner's passion for the lawyer's retirement will not be a successful strategy by itself. Search for "Seven steps to persuasion" for more on this background material.

- Importance of Professional Reputation—If the lawyer is one who remains aware of the value of a well-earned reputation in practice, the partner can discuss steps to protect the lawyer's reputation at the end of the career. Finding the methods to encourage the lawyer to take productive steps such as teaming up with the newer lawyers, sharing mentorship skills, referring more difficult and more taxing cases to others in the firm, and working on nonlegal community matters in the role of elder advisor may help.

- Family Support—Does the lawyer have family supporting a retirement plan or objecting to the possible loss of income or increased time in the home? Family can make an important difference in the process.

- Financial Situation—What is the lawyer's financial situation? Did the firm have a retirement plan such as a 401(k) or SEP-IRA plan in place to set aside funds for retirement?

Most small firms do not generate the cash flow to fund a lawyer's retirement out of current revenues or have partners who think that reducing their take-home pay by the amount going to the retired lawyer is what they signed on for, many with their retirement plans just years away.

- Of Counsel Status—Depending on state practice rules, taking an "of counsel" status in a firm allows for the lawyer to start the move to retirement in a graceful way, at an earlier stage. The lawyer generally steps out of the partnership role, becomes an employee of the remaining partners, and works on some agreeable compensation model.
- Testing—Some bar associations have provided links to the Self-Administered Gerocognitive Exam (SAGE), an online test that may assist in identifying early signs of impairment.

So, the partners have a task ahead of them. Let's look at several strategies.

## Strategy 1: Plan Early

The most important strategy is for the whole firm to start the retirement planning before it is too late. We have all met the family who wished that a parent had timely planned his or her estate. We have to do the same in our law firms in order to protect our practices.

How early is early enough? It depends on the lawyer and the partner. If the lawyer is aware of concerns and is agreeable to working out a mutually beneficial retirement plan, that would be the best alternative. If the practice is profitable enough to fill a retirement account for each lawyer and staff member in the firm, that is even better. Few firms can do that, in part because few can determine when a lawyer's retirement account is "full enough."

Traditionally the law firms that avoid major problems are working on this issue at least five years before the lawyer is expected to hang up the law license and leave the firm.

Partnership discussions should be taking place, and cases that will extend beyond arbitrary intermediate dates should be referred or co-counsel brought in.

Major clients should be introduced to younger lawyers in the firm, and younger lawyers should start to identify with those clients, get familiar with their business opportunities, and take on ownership of the lawyer's book of business. This transition is tricky, and younger lawyers need to exercise negotiation skills in order to maintain a proper role of support and assistance for the lawyer but also become essential for the client.

## Strategy 2: The Partnership Agreement or Retirement Contract

The best plan is one we regularly see in large firms: the contractual retirement. You join the firm with the understanding that you retire no later than the firm's stated retirement age, usually 65 or 70. Some firms have postretirement opportunities, where the decision about those opportunities is made by the remaining partners, not by the aging lawyer. Most lawyers are not kept, since keeping many would undermine the retirement policy and could cause litigation with some disgruntled former partners.

Postretirement benefits may include office space and partial staff, or it could be an offer to serve the firm in an "of counsel" status with malpractice or health insurance coverage. Some firms share fees with the lawyer at a reduced rate, while other firms change the locks and adjust the list of lawyers on the website. A few throw retirement parties to let clients know that the retirement has occurred and the remaining lawyers are ready to work with the clients of the beloved retiree.

This contractual retirement plan usually is clear—it both allows and forces a lawyer to prepare for retirement from that firm and usually avoids serious disputes, since the plan's terms and the firm's culture support each other. The lawyer may have been involved in creating the plan for even older lawyers, so there are no surprises to the lawyer.

The stated retirement plan can be counterproductive. One firm retires all lawyers at age 65 and cannot get agreement to move that age. In the 1950s when the age-65 limit was adopted, lawyers' lifespans and careers were shorter. This firm now sees lawyers still in their prime earning range walking out to a new firm or to a solo practice with a book of business that the firm expected to keep and may have considered that it paid for in retirement benefits.

If you don't have a contract and have waited until the lawyer is over 60 years old, you are likely late for the opportunity to plan early enough. After age 60, each step taken by the partners to discuss the lawyer's retirement could be seen by the lawyer as a move toward eviction or a grab for his or her book of clients. Depending on the attitude of the lawyer, it may mean there are tough times ahead for the law firm.

Contractual plans entered late in a career need to have clear terms and fair consideration for both parties in order to succeed. Don't forget the lawyer is probably an experienced negotiator and may still be clever enough to hire good counsel to assist in negotiating what the older lawyer sees as a buy-out contract with a parachute of gold.

The contract negotiations do not need to be adversarial, but some tension is to be expected by both sides of the negotiations. The parties are talking about money, the purchase and sales price that they are thereafter bound to. The lawyer gets the sales price and the firm pays the purchase price. Most likely there are not extra funds in the firm to pay the full price, so the parties need to make sure that the price paid works for both sides. The selling lawyer is not helped if the firm goes bust paying the contract or loses the clients that will be required to remain in order to afford the payments.

# Strategy 3: When Other Strategies Are Not Working

So what does a firm of younger partners do when the aging lawyer suffers from hardheadedness and refuses to discuss retirement? They may be ready to dissolve the firm, set the lawyer adrift on an ice floe, and move on, but there are intermediate steps that may be more profitable. Losing the lawyer's clients who are loyal to their longtime lawyer and may have stories of their own of being pushed out of business, or showing a lack of stability to the current and future clients, is not the better option yet. And pushing the lawyer too hard will cause you to lose that piece of history of the firm's existence.

## *Bring in the Children*

A discussion with family members may help. In one case, the son of a prominent lawyer, who was also a very good lawyer but not in the firm, took the lead in discussing the future for the aging lawyer. The son started talking to the lawyer about moving on with life, getting to undone projects while the lawyer's health permitted. That was a help to the partners, although not enough by itself.

In another case, the child laid things on the line with an aging solo lawyer, telling the lawyer that in light of deteriorating skills, the child was not going to serve as the IT person, bookkeeper, and gofer for the lawyer. The child, not a lawyer, was much more comfortable reminding the parent of mistakes that had been made and potential ethical violations that had been committed.

## *Enlist the Spouse's Help*

Most lawyers' spouses have high regard for the work the lawyer did. In one matter, the partners reminded the lawyer and spouse of the great reputation the lawyer and spouse had in the community and then shared with the spouse a few practice issues to let her know that the lawyer's reputation was at risk if a few complaining clients were to talk much.

### Confront the Issues Head On

Start having meetings with the lawyer where deficiencies are discussed instead of "fixed" by the partners. Issues such as missed appointment dates, unsent billings, and nonexistent or improper expectations of the office staff all must be discussed at the time that they occur. Partners getting calls from clients who are rightfully upset about their lawyer's problems in case management, memory, or client care is an entirely proper issue to discuss and should lead to full and honest conversations about proper remedies, including the timing of the lawyer's retirement.

### Upping the Ante

If the lawyer does not or cannot engage in honest conversations on the issues, the partner will need to "up the ante" on the discussions of retirement and the alternatives to retirement. More is said below about the alternatives.

The partner has a duty of loyalty to the firm's clients, and in that duty is the lawyer's responsibility to assure that the clients are getting competent legal services. Ignoring the growing deficiencies of a member of the law firm is not fulfilling the fiduciary duty owed to those clients by the lawyer or the partners. Studying and implementing the resolutions and tactics will take more time than it should, so every delay in starting the process will put the firm at risk of client dissatisfaction and malpractice issues.

### Realize There Is No Way Out of the Issue

One aspect of going into a partnership is the understanding that the partnership will end one day. It may end with a planned retirement party, an unexpected death of a partner, a firm breakup, or a forced retirement. Planning and working toward the celebration of a retirement party takes years of work and cooperation. It takes some trust and respect between the lawyer and partners. The unexpected death of a partner is probably the "easiest" way out of the situation but is not recommended for what we hope are friends who have worked hard and had something to live for. It also means that there is a nearly full workload that someone in the law firm must cover while also covering their own caseload.

The law firm breakup ought to be seen as an admission of failure on the part of lawyers who have the skills to put together cooperative ventures for families or businesses or to peacefully dissolve those same ventures for others. It is always more difficult to do that work for yourself, so you may need to engage a lawyer to assist you in making it work. The forced retirement is better than the firm breakup, but only by a matter of degree. The long-lasting scars are evident for those clients who are paying attention, and the pain may erupt at any time. The residual effect on the staff of a breakup or disputed conclusion to a firm cannot be ignored.

# Tactics

When the strategies for a peaceful and quiet implementation of a retirement or succession plan are not working, then the partner may have to change to a new series of tactics. Building on the strategy of confronting the issue head on, the partner may have to focus on saving the practice, and the partner's license, in light of the fiduciary duties owed to the firm's clients.

## Proving the Case

Starting a list of client complaints, engaging in discussions with the professional liability carrier's loss recovery agent, and reviewing the lawyer's finished and unfinished client files for errors or omissions is hard work but meets your burden as a partner and firm member. Make the discussion about the quality of work being done for the lawyer's clients; avoid talking about age or age-related issues other than quality.

Taking the concerns list to the lawyer and engaging in a full and meaningful discussion when a potential firm breakup is on the table as a worst-case solution may get the attention that is needed to get everyone focused on the serious quality issues. Denial of quality problems by the lawyer is more difficult when the list of concerns is on the table and can be referred to as needed.

One concern is that the clients and vendors who mention the issues to the partners are often friends and colleagues of the lawyer. As such, they prefer not to be named as the source of complaints and could be ongoing clients and vendors of the firm, so the partner will want to protect their identities. The lawyer will not appreciate that he or she cannot dispute the words of unnamed sources.

## Countering the Defenses

The lawyer will likely offer several defenses to the partners during the proof of the case. "I started the firm while you were in diapers" response is one for a founder of the firm, especially if the firm has family members involved. While several diaper-related responses may come to mind, keeping the discussion based on the quality of legal work today is the better course.

A memory challenge may occur, which opens the door to agreeing to a test for skills. Neuropsychologists have the ability to test for diminished skills, but you want to assure that the testing is done to determine the level of professional skills. A test that says the lawyer has skills at a level of 120% of the average 80-year-old does not answer whether the lawyer is skilled enough to continue in the practice of law. While the SAGE test mentioned above may be of assistance in some cases, more likely the lawyer will need the informed opinion of a qualified medical professional.

## Intervention

Some firms have staged interventions in the lawyer's career by bringing in local judges, family members, partners, and medical personnel. Many of these have been reported as successful but challenging for the participants. Care must be taken in discussing the lawyer's successes, since the lawyer may not see that all the events occurred years ago, and there are no current successes discussed. Again, the quality of legal services provided needs to be the focus.

## Protecting the Reputation

Part of the problem for the lawyers who are suffering diminished skills is that clients continue to come for legal work. The clients are undercutting the efforts of those with a duty to protect the client and to resolve the lawyer's need to leave the practice. One tactic that may be helpful is to remind the lawyer of the value of the reputation that brings the old clients and friends to see him. There are two legitimate threats to the lawyer's reputation; one is loss of a reputation for quality, while the other is loss of reputation due to professional negligence and the notoriety that comes with such a suit.

Reminding lawyers of those professionals who have lost their reputation for doing quality work due to age-related issues and their need to avoid that damage as they approach the end of their career may be an effective tactic if they are able to recognize the issues.

# Increasing Problem for the Profession

As the Boomers age through the profession, we will see an ever-greater need to address this issue with more successes.

- People are living longer and expect to live even longer.
- Lawyers want to stay active and important throughout their lives.

- The idea of retirement is tied up in the Who/What issue mentioned above. Many do not have a significant life as something other than a lawyer.
- Finances are often not as healthy as the lawyers expected early in their career, and they may not perceive a life without their earnings to be as successful as they have always dreamed.
- There are not any easy solutions to these problems. JLAP groups are working to find effective ways to ease the transition, but the groups have not found all the tools quite yet.

Time to solve these issues is running short for some of us lawyers. This may leave the heavy lifting to the younger partners or the millennial lawyers; I don't see them coming up with easy answers anytime soon.

# Part III

# Maintaining Ties with the Bar

---

Leaving the active practice of law doesn't necessarily mean that lawyers have to surrender that hard-earned license to practice and stop participating in activities of the organized bar.

---

**Chapter 9**

The Bar Is Our Home
*Marvin S.C. Dang*

**Chapter 10**

Maintaining Your Status with the Bar
*Craig A. Stokes*

# 9

## The Bar Is Our Home

*by Marvin S.C. Dang*

It's been said that "home isn't a place, it's a feeling." For many senior lawyers, home is the bar . . . the bar associations. Whether it's a state or local bar association, an affinity bar association, or the American Bar Association, these organizations are the "feel good" homes for many senior lawyers, including me.

ABA lawyer members who are 62 years of age or older or who have been licensed to practice law for 37 or more years are automatically enrolled in the Senior Lawyers Division. There are no additional dues to be an SLD member. (Before 2016, lawyers who were 55 years of age or older could join the SLD by paying dues.) In 2018 about 60,000 lawyers were SLD members. These senior lawyers—or "experienced" lawyers as they are dubbed by the SLD—comprise about one out of every four ABA dues-paying lawyer members.

While many of these experienced lawyers are still working full-time, others are semiretired or retired. They have not only remained ABA members; many continue to be active volunteers in the SLD and in various ABA sections, divisions, forums, standing and special committees, and commissions. These volunteers serve in leadership positions, write books and articles, speak at continuing education programs and webinars, and participate in myriad committee activities. And these experienced lawyers are volunteering past their 60s and into their 70s and 80s.

I asked six experienced lawyers in 2018 to share some of their perspectives and to explain why they continue to volunteer in bar activities. Those lawyers are:

- **John Hardin "Jack" Young,** of Rehoboth Beach, Delaware, who has been a lawyer for 45 years. He's semiretired and is "of counsel" to the Sandler Reiff law firm.
- San Francisco lawyer **John Uilkema** passed the bar 57 years ago and is semiretired from the law firm of Dergosits and Noah.
- Admitted to the California bar 58 years ago, **Charles "Chuck" Collier** fully retired last year after most recently being a partner emeritus at a law firm.
- **Louraine Arkfeld,** of Tempe, Arizona, is a retired judge. A licensed lawyer for 41 years, she now consults and teaches.
- A lawyer for 50 years, **Al Harvey** works full-time as "of counsel" to the Lewis Thomason firm in Memphis, Tennessee.
- **Ruth Kleinfeld,** of Manchester, New Hampshire, retired as a judge two years ago and is establishing a part-time arbitration practice. She's been a lawyer for 53 years.

# Decades of ABA Involvement

**Marvin Dang:** I know that all of you are longtime ABA members and have been active volunteers for decades. When did you join the ABA and what ABA activities have you been involved with (besides the Senior Lawyers Division)?

**Jack Young:** I joined the ABA in 1973 upon admission to the Virginia bar. In the ABA I've been Chair of the Standing Committee on Election Law; Chair of the Election Law Task Force of the Section of International Law; and Chair of the Section of Administrative Law and Regulatory Practice. I served on the ABA Board of Governors.

**John Uilkema:** I became an ABA member in 1961. I was Chair and Honorary Council Member of the Section of Intellectual Property Law (IPL); IPL Section Delegate to the ABA House of Delegates; ABA Board of Governors member; ABA Nominating Committee member; Council member of the Section of Civil Rights and Social Justice; and Chair of the ABA Standing Committee on Group and Prepaid Legal Services.

**Chuck Collier:** I joined in 1974. I was on the ABA Board of Governors.

**Louraine Arkfeld:** In 1977 I became an ABA member when I graduated from law school. I dropped out for a few years and rejoined in 1984. I'm currently Chair of the ABA Commission on Law and Aging. I was Chair of the ABA Judicial Division; Judicial Member-at-Large on the ABA Board of Governors; Chair of the National Conference of Specialized Court Judges; and Council member of the Section of International Law.

**Al Harvey:** I joined the ABA in 1968. I've been actively involved with the Section of Litigation; the Solo, Small Firm, and General Practice Division; the Civil Rights and Social Justice Section; the ABA Retirement Funds Board; and the ABA Standing Committee on Law and National Security.

**Ruth Kleinfeld:** I became an ABA member in 1983. I've been Chair of the National Conference of Administrative Law Judiciary (NCALJ); liaison from NCALJ to the ABA Commission on Women in the Profession; and liaison from the Judicial Division to the ABA Commission on Law and Aging.

**Dang:** When did you join the ABA Senior Lawyers Division, what SLD activities are you currently involved with, and what are some of your past activities?

**Young:** I've been an SLD member since 2010. I'm currently Immediate Past Chair of the SLD; Chair of the Nominating Committee; Co-Chair of the Opioid Initiative Task Force; and SLD liaison to the Rule of Law Initiative. I was SLD Chair (2017–2018); Planning Committee member of the SLD's 2018 Opioid Summit; Chair of the Continuing Legal Education Committee; Chair of the Non-Dues Revenue Committee; and Chair of the Alternative Dispute Resolution Committee.

**Uilkema:** I became a member in 2005. I'm Co-Chair of the 2019 Annual Meeting Committee; Co-Chair of the Member Benefits Committee; SLD liaison to the ABA Section of Civil Rights and Social Justice; and liaison from the Intellectual Property Law Section to the SLD. Previously I served as a member of the SLD Council; member of the Annual Meeting Committee; and Membership Committee Chair.

**Collier:** It was around 2000 or 2001 that I became an SLD member. Currently I'm Chair of the SLD's Supreme Court Trip Committee and Special Advisor to the Book Publishing Board. I was SLD Chair (2008–2009); Chair or Co-Chair of the SLD's *Experience* magazine editorial board; Chair or Co-Chair of the SLD Supreme Court Trip Committee; and Chair of the Book Publishing Board. I've written reviews of SLD books for *Experience* magazine.

**Arkfeld:** I joined the SLD in 2010. I'm currently Vice-Chair of the Opioid Initiative Task Force; Co-Chair of the Strategic Planning Committee; and SLD liaison to the ABA Commission on Law and Aging. I was SLD Chair (2015–2016); SLD Council member; and Chair of the Transition Task Force.

**Harvey:** I became an SLD member around 1999. I'm Chair-Elect of the SLD. Previously I was SLD Vice Chair, Delegate to the ABA House of Delegates, on the SLD Council, and a member of the SLD Ethics Committee.

**Kleinfeld:** It was in 1995. I'm currently a Delegate from the SLD to the ABA House of Delegates, Chair of SLD Travel Committee, and Co-Chair of Pickering Award and Reception Committee. I was SLD Chair and Immediate Past Chair. I've been involved with travel, Annual Meeting dinners, writing for *Voice of Experience*, the By-Laws Committee, and webinars.

**Dang:** Currently, how much of your time per month do your ABA activities take?

**Young:** Currently about 5 hours a month.

**Uilkema:** It varies, but at present I would estimate 15 to 20 hours per month.

**Collier:** The amount of time varies, but probably in the range of 5 to 10 hours per month.

**Arkfeld:** Depending on what I have been involved in, the time has varied from 10 hours a week to 10 hours a month.

**Harvey:** My ABA activities take about 50+ hours of time per month.

**Kleinfeld:** I estimate about 10 hours a month. For each ABA Annual Meeting and Midyear Meeting there's about 7 to 8 days plus travel time.

# Reasons to Stay Involved

**Dang:** Why do you choose to stay actively involved with the SLD and with other ABA activities?

**Young:** It's the sense of connection with the legal profession, the continuing legal education, and the camaraderie of the profession.

**Uilkema:** The activities and their objectives are important to me. But probably even more important are the friends and personal relationships that they have fostered.

**Collier:** I enjoy bar association work and enjoy working with other successful lawyers and judges. I also hope that my efforts are of assistance to other lawyers through publications, committee work, etc., and contribute to the legal profession.

**Arkfeld:** I enjoy the opportunity to be involved in meaningful work and to stay engaged in current issues. I continue to meet interesting people and enjoy professional colleagues who share my interests.

**Harvey:** It's the professional responsibility, service to the bar and the community, social interaction—being with friends built over a lifetime as a lawyer, enjoyment of bar work and activities, and travel.

**Kleinfeld:** I enjoy the friendship and interaction with intelligent, successful, and interesting lawyers and judges. Staying active in the bar association helps me maintain competence and social utility and the opportunity for multigenerational interaction.

**Dang:** What would you tell a senior lawyer who has been active in bar activities (especially ABA and SLD) are the reasons that he or she should stay actively involved?

**Young:** I would give all the reasons in my earlier response.

**Uilkema:** I would tell them that all the good things that have been important to them . . . educational opportunities, experiences, and friendships . . . will continue. Also, there's good and important information for them relating to the law practice, the slowdown of the law practice, and retirement.

**Collier:** Exiting from full-time practice opens up so many opportunities to utilize one's skills and contribute to the profession through committee work, writing, speaking, and mentoring. Staying active in a bar association allows one to continue to work with friends and colleagues and to render services to the profession and the community. It gives a person the chance to share his or her expertise with others.

**Arkfeld:** I would repeat my reasons in my earlier response.

**Harvey:** The same reasons as in my earlier response.

**Kleinfeld:** Friendships, intellectual stimulation, meaningful work, and ability to contribute to the vitality of the organized bar. Some ABA members have told me they stay members mainly for insurance coverage benefits. Also, the ABA offers many economic benefits.

# It's Never Too Late to Get Involved

**Dang:** What would you tell a senior lawyer who isn't currently active in bar activities are the reasons that she or he should now consider getting involved?

**Young:** The SLD in particular provides an opportunity to stay involved in the profession, to continue to work on projects of interest, and to receive information important to life and wellness decisions for yourself, your family, and your friends.

**Uilkema:** You'll find the activities and your involvement satisfying, educational, and useful, and, probably even more importantly, you will enjoy the people you meet and the friendships you develop. Somewhat ironically, I have often made closer personal friends in my bar activities than I have from my law partnerships. In retrospect, I recall my much older and first senior partner who had been the chair of the ABA Section of Intellectual Property and who obviously experienced the same thing. At that time I didn't understand it and was somewhat envious of his ABA friends.

**Collier:** The benefits of bar association work include the opportunity to write articles and books; the chance to participate in special events at the ABA such as the annual meeting; hearing great speakers and the leaders of the profession; networking; continuing friendships over many more years; staying involved in the profession; and contributing through committee work.

**Arkfeld:** I would tell her or him the reasons I stated earlier. Also if you no longer have a professional workplace, it's difficult to have these opportunities without something like the ABA.

**Harvey:** I would give the same reasons that I gave earlier.

**Kleinfeld:** It's the intellectual stimulation and the opportunity to contribute by giving back to the legal profession.

**Dang:** How easy is it for a senior lawyer who hasn't been involved to now get involved in bar activities?

**Young:** The SLD is open to all ABA members who are 62 years of age or older. It has a place for everyone at all levels of involvement. It's open to participation in each of its substantive committees, as well as being open to new projects and ideas.

**Uilkema:** It would seem very easy, but for the person who has never been involved, that person might have a built-in resistance to getting involved.

**Collier:** There are always openings on committees that make it very easy to get actively involved. Every volunteer is welcome.

**Arkfeld:** It's easy to get involved because organizations are always looking for people willing to do good work.

**Harvey:** The first step could be as easy as attending a meeting or joining a committee.

**Kleinfeld:** It's very easy if the lawyer is willing to do the work (write, attend meetings, or present a webinar). It's also easy if you get introduced by a friend or associate.

**Dang:** How can senior lawyers be actively involved with bar activities without having to travel to meetings?

**Young:** Attending ABA or SLD meetings can be the least important part of membership—although the meetings are both fun and interesting. Senior lawyers can be actively involved through writing articles for the SLD's monthly *Voice of Experience* e-newsletter or the quarterly *Experience* magazine, participating in webinars and CLE programs, or drafting resolutions to the House of Delegates on issues important to you that you believe the House of Delegates (through sponsorship by the SLD) should enact.

**Uilkema:** They can get involved through developing some kind of personal involvement that makes them feel a part of the process. It's important that they are involved with other people.

**Collier:** Senior lawyers can be involved through e-mail and telephone. Many SLD committee members participate only by phone and e-mail.

**Arkfeld:** They can be involved without travel because many SLD committees work online or via conference call. The SLD is always looking for good writers for articles for the *Voice of Experience* e-newsletter or *Experience* magazine, and this work can be done remotely.

**Harvey:** Most committees work via conference calls and email. But to be really active, they should plan to attend some meetings or conferences.

**Kleinfeld:** Without attending meetings, they can participate in committee meetings by telephone, write for the *Voice of Experience* e-newsletter or for *Experience* magazine, or participate as presenter at webinars (this can be done remotely).

## Some Final Thoughts

**Dang:** Do you have any other comments?

**Young:** Yes, senior lawyers have a lot to contribute based on their experience and their experiences. The SLD is an excellent place to continue to connect to the law and the bar. In the words of Monty

Python in *Monty Python and the Holy Grail*: "I'm not dead yet." Anything but. Senior lawyers are a vital part of the legal profession.

**Uilkema:** The SLD should keep up the good work!

**Collier:** The SLD is a strong, vigorous ABA entity. Anyone active in it will benefit from participation in its activities.

**Arkfeld:** I am always reinvigorated after engaging with my SLD colleagues!

**Harvey:** Enjoyment of service to the profession should not stop on retirement. The need is there at every level, and experience gained through a life in the law is still valuable.

**Kleinfeld:** Get involved!

Continued bar association work is not just for the good of the legal profession. It's good for those who volunteer. The ABA in general, and the SLD specifically, has been and continues to be the "feel good" home for Jack, John, Chuck, Louraine, Al, Ruth, and me. The bar can continue to be—or begin to be—the home for many other senior, experienced lawyers.

# 10

# Maintaining Your Status with the Bar

*by Craig A. Stokes*

The list taped to the wall at the state supreme court clerk's office or at the law school. The continuously refreshed board of bar examiners' results webpage. The phone call from a friend followed by the phone call to the bar examiners' office. The bar examiners' letter (fat or thin envelope). Few moments are more etched into a lawyer's memory than the moment when she received her bar exam results. The thought of ever needing to undergo the bar examination process again can be daunting. A lawyer considering a career shift must decide what she is going to do with her law license if she leaves active practice. The possibility of repeating the bar exam process may weigh in the decision-making process of the lawyer who is considering a transition. Few current lawyers would want to leave themselves exposed to another bar exam if their non-legal career choice did not work out.

The decision to keep a law license active or not is not only emotional, avoiding the risk of another bar exam, but also economic. Most jurisdictions require continuing legal education, an investment of time and money. Some of those jurisdictions have strict limits on the number of on-demand or distance learning hours, limits that require physical attendance at one or more seminars.

Add to that the cost of bar dues and, in some cases such as Tennessee, the professional license fees. Many states have Client Security Fund assessments, and Oregon at least has a mandatory legal malpractice fund charge.

It is not possible within the scope of this chapter to outline all possible alternatives in each state. But we will highlight some of the alternatives for lawyers who may choose to explore other options while keeping their foot inside the door of legal practice. The admonition of many judges to counsel, "Did you read the rules," rings particularly true when a lawyer is considering a change from active status on a law license.

The definitions of "retired" and "inactive" status and ability to change out of such status are not uniform among jurisdictions. A lawyer who is seeking to put law practice on hold for a while cannot merely rely upon the label that a state uses to describe its various licensing statuses. While many jurisdictions have adopted uniform laws in many areas, the rules for alternatives to active legal practice are more varied than those for admission to the bar and reciprocity. Between reciprocity, the Uniform Bar Examination, and its various components, states are starting to converge in their gateways to legal practice. Be forewarned, however; the portals to the anterooms on the edge of active legal practice and reentry in the various jurisdictions are not identical or converging.

## Continued Active Status

The costs of maintaining one's license are the state supreme court's and/or state bar's dues and the cost and time to maintain CLE status. In a few states, like Alabama, Tennessee, and Texas, the cost of the state occupational license for lawyers is an additional cost of keeping one's license active. However, a few states do reduce the fees of active status for older lawyers, such as Idaho's reduced fee for lawyers 65 years of age and older. South Carolina grants lawyers 60 years of age or older with 30 years of practice an exemption from annual CLE requirements. However, those lawyers contemplating testing out another career may want to seek to step away from CLE, bar dues, client security fund assessments, and in some cases mandatory malpractice insurance assessments.

Lawyers who want to avoid the annual costs of a law license and the time and cost of CLE but by reason of age cannot qualify for one of these exemptions must examine their jurisdiction's rules.

# Retirement

Unlike perhaps 50 years ago, the word "retirement" has less to do with age and more to do with factors such as a career transition or a desire to decamp to the woods for self-discovery. A lawyer considering "retirement" from the legal profession must consult with his or her own bar's definition of what retirement status means for the license and the lawyer's potential reentry into the legal system.

Ohio recognizes fully retired status for lawyers. However, retirement from law practice in the state of Ohio is an irrevocable decision. The state's supreme court flatly states that a lawyer who wants to keep the door open to future practice must seek inactive rather than retired status. Retirement in Ohio means another bar exam for the retired lawyer who changes her mind.

Colorado allows lawyers over age 65 take inactive status, equivalent to retirement, without payment of annual fees. Those who seek inactive status prior to age 65 must pay an annual fee. Colorado's inactive status for those over age 65 is effectively retirement status, without the use of the word "retirement."

Pennsylvania limits the period of "retirement" to three years if the lawyer seeks reinstatement to active status. The retired lawyer must pay prior assessments for the period of retired status.

In lieu of "retired" status, Wisconsin offers an "emeritus" status that is the best of all worlds. A lawyer who is 70 or older and has actively practiced the prior two years may file a request for emeritus status that results in waiver of bar dues, supreme court assessments, and CLE requirements. The only charge that an emeritus lawyer must pay in Wisconsin is to the Lawyer's Fund for Client Protection.

# "Inactive" Status

In most jurisdictions, inactive status just suspends CLE requirements and reduces bar dues. The pathway back to active practice for the lawyer who repents of her decision to go inactive is simply taking catch-up CLE for the compliance years of inactive practice. But in some jurisdictions the pathway back to active practice is not so easy.

Some states, such as North Carolina, flatly do not have a "retired" status but rather permit lawyers who would otherwise seek retired status to become inactive. Bar dues must be paid for the year of conversion to inactive status. The state's bar allows seven years of inactive status, with years in military service or active status in another state's bar excluded from the calculation of the seven years. The danger to the North Carolina lawyer who remains in inactive status for more than the seven years that are counted is that the now-former lawyer must sit for another bar exam to resume active practice. North Carolina has scaled requirements for reinstatement to active status depending on the period, with longer periods of inactive status requiring a character investigation.

Like North Carolina, Idaho scales up requirements for reentry to active practice depending on the time that the Idaho lawyer has been inactive. For the first four years, the reinstatement requirement is only CLE. Starting at the fifth year, the lawyer must submit to character and fitness investigation and submit fingerprints. Those who are inactive more than seven years may be required to take all or part of the bar examination, and those whose inactive state exceeds ten years must start the entire bar admission process again.

New Mexico also places some substantial burdens on the lawyer who seeks active status after inactivity. The applicant must pay

$350, file an application for reinstatement, which is a bar examination application, and pay an investigation fee. For those such as the author who first completed a bar examination application back in 1980, the depth and detail of current bar examination application forms compared to those of decades ago will come as a shock. That alone might deter a lawyer from seeking inactive status in New Mexico.

Washington state suspends CLE for inactive lawyers; depending on the number of years of inactive status, it requires makeup of some missed CLE; and if the lawyer's period of inactive status exceeds six years, the lawyer must take a reinstatement course.

California has one of the simplest requirements for reinstatement to active status: file an application with a fingerprint card and pay the current year's dues. The annual dues of $155 for inactive California bar status are a relatively inexpensive way to keep one's options open for recommencing active legal practice.

## Conclusion

The paths out of and back into active legal practice are as varied as the number of jurisdictions. The lawyer who wants to keep her options open to active legal practice must read carefully her jurisdiction's rules for the type of status she needs to maintain to keep the doors of the legal profession open to her. There are different costs for the various possible options to active license status, and there may be time periods after which the decision to leave active legal practice becomes irrevocable. The economic costs, both in dollars and time, should be counted along with the possible anxiety, or perhaps liberation, of a potential final exit from law practice. For some, the thought of possibly facing another bar examination and the post-exam waiting ritual, along with possible time limits on reentry, might weigh in favor of maintaining active status.

# Part IV

# Taking Work in Different Directions

A second act doesn't have to mean an "all or nothing" approach or even "business as usual." Changing the kind of law you practice and shifting the delivery mode, and even the business model, can open new windows of opportunity.

**Chapter 11**

Morphing to Mediation: ADR as an Alternative
*David J. Abeshouse*

**Chapter 12**

What Should I Do with What I Know?
*Lisa A. Runquist*

**Chapter 13**

Pro Bono Work after Retiring
*Joan M. Burda*

95

# 11

# Morphing to Mediation: ADR as an Alternative

*by David J. Abeshouse*

Lawyers are not known to be an especially satisfied bunch. Without attempting to decipher the various factors underlying this phenomenon, one safely can say that at a certain point mid-career, many, if not most, lawyers consider their options for their future paths: continue on the same course; scale back; change specialties or focus; start or join a sideline business; teach instead of or in addition to practicing; ditch law practice altogether; or mix it up in other ways.

Although I was not desperate for a change, I also was not satisfied with maintaining the status quo, so I ended up adopting an amalgam of most of these paths. I hope that my personal story of morphing from business litigation lawyer to alternative dispute resolution (ADR) neutral might benefit in some way those who may seek to change their practices and lives.

I should clarify at the outset that this discussion is oriented generally toward the commercial ADR realm rather than matrimonial, community, or other ADR disciplines about which I lack experience and knowledge and which I understand are quite distinct from the commercial world.

"Born" a commercial litigator, I recognized early on many of the foibles of court litigation and our generally broken court system, so I eagerly accepted assignments in ADR matters, principally arbitration and mediation. I gained experience and expertise in business-to-business arbitration and mediation (aka B2B ADR) over a period of years as a lawyer-advocate for my clients, first as an associate (in the 1980s) and then as a partner throughout the 1990s in a law firm. I spent an appreciable amount of my time as a commercial litigation department lawyer handling the related commercial arbitrations and mediations that came to us and realized that I substantially preferred the more streamlined, sensible, efficient, and yet still rigorous practice that ADR engendered, in contrast to litigating in the state and federal courts.

During this time, I not only took every opportunity I could to handle arbitrations and mediations at my law firm, but I also embarked on a conscious course of taking as many ADR CLE classes and trainings as possible to broaden and deepen my knowledge of ADR. The CLE classes enhanced my skills as a lawyer-advocate representing clients in ADR matters, and the trainings enhanced my skills as a budding neutral arbitrator and mediator. I did not simply take a 40-hour training course in arbitration and a 40-hour training course in mediation and call it a day. Over the years, I took several of those multi-day trainings in both mediation and arbitration offered by different providers and many hundreds of hours of CLE coursework in both areas.

In 2000, not long after I'd begun to serve as a neutral arbitrator and mediator, I left my equity partnership in the law firm and went "true solo," in large measure so I could practice the way I wanted to. That meant gradually weaning off the remunerative spigot of commercial litigation in court and increasing the mix of ADR cases in the advocacy side of my practice. Ultimately, I ceased doing court work and devoted my law practice exclusively to ADR, while also continuing to grow the proportion of neutral work relative to lawyering.

I achieved the first goal, cessation of court work, by 2009 or 2010. With that initial morphing complete, I turned to the next transformation: Nowadays, I spend more than 80% of my time as a neutral arbitrator, neutral mediator, or ADR law consultant and less than 20% of my time as an ADR lawyer representing parties in commercial arbitration or mediation. That's the ideal mix for me at present, for several reasons. Continuing to practice law at least a bit (i) reassures some lawyers who select their arbitrators and mediators that I keep current in the law and am not doing neutral work as a half-hearted retirement career, (ii) allows me to be very selective in which cases I take on as an advocate so that they're cases and clients I truly want to handle, and (iii) if there were a drastic downturn in work as an ADR neutral, it'd be easier for me to ramp up the legal work to fill more of my time. The realm of the neutral offers no guarantees; indeed, most of my colleagues would agree that neutral work is characterized by unpredictable peaks and valleys.

Between the extensive coursework I've taken and my real-life experience as a lawyer and neutral, I developed enough expertise to speak at approximately 100 classes and trainings over the past decade and a half and write many articles, book chapters, and other published works. I spent many hours each week for nearly two decades engaging in extensive business and legal networking activities (founding a couple of networking groups, belonging to a number of others, attending open events of other groups to which I did not belong but to which I was invited, meeting in person or by phone with many contacts each month, and numerous other efforts), so I met thousands of people on whom I could call or who could call on me. I also developed a virtual network of legal and business contacts through participation for several years in the ABA's Solosez listserv, joining LinkedIn in 2004 as soon as it emerged from beta, and other online avenues.

I made it a point to be as responsive as possible to those who did call on me, for whatever reason, and that became a hallmark

of my professional philosophy. See, for example, www.Responsive
Lawyer.com and www.ResponsiveAttorney.com (I easily obtained
those web domain names in around 2006–2007, when there were
approximately 1.2 million lawyers in the United States and the
profession had maintained an active web presence for about a
decade; this was so easy because no one else had either thought
of it or valued it sufficiently as a concept). These two URLs redi-
rect to my main website (which should be updated before the next
millennium).

Each of these many elements has contributed in some way
toward helping me on the path to a more satisfying career. Some
of these elements might work for others, some might not; I've
always felt that one need not attempt to fit the proverbial square
peg into a round hole. Rather, do what comes naturally, do what
you do well, and you're more likely to succeed.

So, at this point in my metamorphosis, I've adopted a bit of
each of the options mentioned at the outset:

- I've continued on the same course as before to some extent,
  but I've decreased the amount of lawyering I do in favor of
  serving as a neutral, which now consumes the vast majority of my professional time.

- I've scaled back considerably in some ways, and not so
  much in others: I do no court litigation, less representation
  of parties in business ADR cases, and far less business and
  legal networking than I used to do, but I still work relatively long hours each day and probably too many days
  each year. My consolation is that I greatly enjoy the work
  that I do—I'd rather do "too much" of what I like than
  work less but at something that I dislike.

- I've changed focus to the extent that I've relinquished my
  court-based practice and devote my time exclusively to
  commercial ADR matters, principally as a neutral; moreover, as I decreased and then dropped commercial litigation, I have replaced it with a focus on serving as a neutral

in international arbitrations and mediations. I greatly enjoy the emphasis on international ADR work that I have developed over the past decade.

- I started two small sideline businesses directly related to my main concentration: The first, admittedly somewhat short-lived, was a negotiation workshop that I began with a partner. We're still friends, but the mildly successful business venture did not last. More significantly, I serve as ADR law consultant to litigators and business transactional lawyers. I help experienced trial lawyers navigate the unfamiliar waters of arbitration proceedings, translating from the languages of FRCP, FRE, and CPLR into the language of the Commercial Arbitration Rules of the forum providers and assisting counsel in strategizing within this new context, including dealing appropriately with the forum personnel. I help experienced business transactional lawyers—who rarely get involved in handling disputes—draft meaningful and strategic dispute resolution clauses for their business agreements, both domestically and internationally. They all are amazed at how much they need to learn, so it is rewarding for me to be the instrument providing that assistance.

- I experimented with returning to academia as an adjunct professor of law teaching ADR law at a New York–area law school, and although I enjoyed it, I found that situation too disruptive to my neutral practice schedule. I might be inclined to try it again some years hence, if I slow down the flow of my neutral work.

So, what of those who are considering venturing into the ADR domain? As mentioned, I have been training new and experienced mediators and arbitrators for several years (on behalf of my state bar and otherwise). Trainees frequently (almost always) ask how they can develop their neutral practices as they acquire skills. So do many others.

In recent years, I've heard colleagues say to me and others that they would like to follow the career path that I've chosen; that I'm a "role model" for reinventing one's legal career; and similar somewhat exaggerated declarations. Nearly every week, I field e-mails and phone calls from colleagues, acquaintances, those who have attended my speaking engagements or read my articles, friends' children who attend or recently graduated from law school, former opposing counsel, and others who want to know how to become more involved in ADR. I try gently to inject a dose of reality at the outset, cautioning that it's harder to accomplish now than in "my day," because, among other things, there's more competition. ADR's growth and popularity have made it a more competitive playing field.

Depending on the experience level of the inquirer, the topics covered often include the following.

The first inquiry should be whether you really are suited to be a mediator or arbitrator. Both of those roles are quite different from being a lawyer, advocating for one's client. Many myths and misconceptions persist about ADR, and it's best to disabuse oneself of them before embarking on a path toward becoming a neutral. So read up, speak with every knowledgeable person you can find, and take all available coursework related to your intended goal.

It may not surprise you that the most established arbitrators and mediators get the most work, but it is important to recognize that as a newbie to the profession, you are likely to be on the lighter end of the work spectrum. Moreover, you may not be able to command the same hourly rate as a neutral as you are accustomed to receiving as a lawyer. Running your neutral practice is a business, but a different sort—with different marketing principles—than running a law practice. If you are to make a go of it, you will have to learn new skills not only as a neutral but also in your new business.

Those who wish to become an arbitrator or mediator should understand that before parties and their counsel will repose trust and confidence in you, you must earn it through years of experience. My gradual personal journey—described above—took a couple of decades before I gained a strong foothold in my chosen field, and it involved all of the elements mentioned. I've always felt that it's the tapestry, rather than any individual thread, that creates the environment for organizing the career you want.

So I recommend doing many of the things that I've done, but I'm not sure that nowadays that would be sufficient. One question to address early on is whether you wish to be an arbitrator, a mediator, or both. Focusing efforts on one rather than both allows for more concentrated progress; however, many neutrals have accomplished careers in both arenas, so it is far from impossible—you would have to decide whether you're more suited to venturing it simultaneously or sequentially. Much depends on your career stage, financial situation, geographic location/marketplace conditions, ability to apply existing skills and experience in a new way and new setting, ability to develop new skills notwithstanding years of reinforced experience, and similar factors.

If you're early on in your career and have several decades ahead of you, you have the benefit of time to undertake many of these efforts and others that suit your needs and personality. By the same token, recognize that it is unlikely that you will start being called on to serve as a neutral very early in your career. Those years are useful for building credibility and preparing yourself to serve going forward. Be sure to maintain a full record of all of the formal educational opportunities of which you've availed yourself, as you may need to report them in future on an application or a profile, and you don't want to lose them to the sands of time. Internships and shadowing experienced neutrals also may be options. You needn't lose hope, however: Some motivated individuals have managed to kick-start their neutral work with not much more than a decade of ADR-focused efforts. Some find it helpful to obtain an advanced degree such as an LLM (Master of Laws) in one of the ADR disciplines. And in recent years, in some settings there has been an increased emphasis on diversity among neutrals, so women and those who are racially diverse may find neutral work a somewhat more welcoming profession than in the past.

One specific suggestion I have proposed, particularly to younger hopefuls, is to spend some time skim-reading the ADR literature: online articles, blogs, books, treatises, whatever you can consume. Soon, you may discover certain aspects or areas in which you have particular interest. Concentrate your reading in these with a view toward finding an author (law firm partner, professor, prominent neutral, ADR forum executive, legal editor) whose work speaks to your interest. Select something about one of this author's works, and write to her insightfully about it. This author might need someone to assist on her next article, and you can offer yourself as an assistant or co-author. You soon might get your first byline and begin to present yourself to the community as knowledgeable about ADR. Being a published author on pertinent ADR topics is a good credential to add to your future application to serve as a neutral.

If you're later in your career, I would caution against considering neutral work as a semiretirement career to be picked up a mere couple of years before one retires—as a general rule, it's not, and it typically takes years of targeted efforts to develop. You should examine your existing assets, such as expertise and professional reputation in a particular subject area or discipline (e.g., cybersecurity, forensic accounting), the network of contacts and relationships that you have developed, and any ADR-related experience (even indirect) you might have amassed. See how you might best apply those assets to advance your aim of establishing yourself as a neutral. Sometimes, those with special abilities (particularly ones that are relatively rare and in demand in the ADR world, such as cybersecurity and forensic accounting) may get fast-tracked into the profession. Notwithstanding your considerable experience, you still must become educated about ADR, so put ego and habit aside—even if you've served in a related capacity, such as a judgeship—and take ADR courses and embrace other learning opportunities wherever possible. Keep track of all formal education you take, as noted above, as you may need to report it in future.

You can take a training course, hang up a shingle proclaiming yourself an arbitrator or mediator, and sit back and see what happens, but the result in that scenario is readily predictable. Great sages throughout time have declared that "anything worth doing is worth doing right" and that "it takes great effort to do worthwhile things." And of course, "Do or do not . . . there is no try" (Yoda). These pronouncements have been passed down through the generations of philosophers (and moviegoers) because they generally are true and encompass good advice. They apply with at least equal force to becoming a neutral.

## Additional Recommended Reading

Douglas E. Noll, *Hey, I'll Just Be a Mediator When I Retire! Not So Fast . . .*, Experience (Mar. 2, 2018), https://www.american bar.org/groups/senior_lawyers/publications/experience/2018 /january-february/hey-ill-just-be-mediator-when-i-retire.html

John Robert Van Winkle, Mediation: A Path Back for the Lost Lawyer (2nd ed. ABA 2005)

Dwight Golann, Sharing a Mediator's Powers: Effective Advocacy in Settlement (ABA 2014)

Jeffrey Krivis & Naomi Lucks, How to Make Money as a Mediator (and Create Value for Everyone) (Jossey-Bass/Wiley 2006)

Tammy Lenski, Making Mediation Your Day Job (3rd ed. MyriaccordMedia 2014)

# 12

# What Should I Do with What I Know?

*by Lisa A. Runquist*

For the past 40-plus years, I have represented nonprofit organizations. I generally like my clients, and I like the fact that I can help the good guys. But frankly, I am getting tired of a lot of the mundane work that comes in. I can draft articles, bylaws, resolutions, and exemption applications practically in my sleep. In fact, these days very little of the work that comes in is interesting enough for me to really want to keep doing it directly. Clearly there is some work that I want to keep doing, such as serving as an expert witness, restructuring complex nonprofit organizations in a way that allows the organization to preserve the purpose even when the directors and officers change, and other similar matters that pique my interest. And I continue to enjoy teaching, speaking, and writing.

But the concept of "retirement" (is that really a word?) brings up several questions. The first is: To whom should I refer the work I don't want to keep doing? I have a generalized practice for a very specific and specialized area of law. Because there are very few lawyers who understand nonprofits, especially religious organizations, making referrals is always a challenge, especially when the potential client is located in another jurisdiction.

There is a second question, which is what this chapter is about: How do I make the knowledge that I have acquired available to other lawyers who either want to make a career of representing nonprofits or simply want to represent their local nonprofit but don't know where to start? If I am successful in answering this second question, then the first can also resolve itself.

Obviously, I can continue to write, speak, and teach. I have written several books, and once I find the time (i.e., when I successfully manage to hand off much of my practice to someone else), I have several other books I want to write. But the problem with writing books is that they are, by necessity, general in nature and may not answer the specific question that the lawyer might have. And the practice of many lawyers, especially those of the millennial generation, is to go online to find their answer, rather than referring to a book.

One of the things I do for many of the classes I teach is to record a short video introduction to each topic. These videos, by their nature, are generic and do not address specific issues. Ah. What would happen if I recorded an entire library of videos that are about five minutes each and address only one particular issue or subissue? Then when lawyers search for their particular concern, they will not have to plow through an entire book to see if they can find the answer or even spend half an hour searching through what appear to be relevant articles to try to find the answer. If they can formulate the question, the answer would be available. If they are not sure what to even ask, they could look through my list of videos and figure out what is relevant or at least where to start. I figure I can easily come up with 500 topics and subtopics as a basic outline.

For example, when someone wants to form a nonprofit organization, some of the initial questions would be:

1.   Should I form a corporation, an unincorporated association, a trust, or a limited liability company? Just with this first question there are many subtopics, including what is

involved in forming each type of entity, how does each type of entity operate, what are the advantages or disadvantages of each, and when would one entity be clearly preferable?

2. In what jurisdiction should the organization be formed? Again, there are subtopics, including why it is often best to form the organization where it will be operating, what the basic differences are among state laws that the lawyer might want to consider, and what types of filings are involved.

3. Who is going to be involved in the formation and operation of the nonprofit? Will you have members? What is the difference between an officer and a director, and how many do you need? Can you pay your directors and officers? How often do you need to have meetings? What type of notice is required?

4. What is the difference between a nonprofit and an exempt organization? What do you have to do to establish the exempt status of the organization?

And on and on.

Once I have put together my outline of topics, I may ask lawyers I know for suggestions of additional topics, as well as feedback on which seem to be the most important topics to be addressed first.

I have also realized that I know a lot of history about how the law came to be the way it is. For example, I can tell you why the California attorney general exercises only limited oversight over religious organizations. Even most of the lawyers who regularly represent nonprofits probably could not give you the answer to that question, since this change in the law occurred before many of them were even born. Another great topic for a short video, containing information not otherwise readily available.

Limiting each video to a specific issue also makes it easier to keep the library up to date. When the law changes, I can simply redo that short video.

I have also thought that it would be good to make available some of the specific written materials that pertain to the particular matter being addressed. In some cases, the materials would cover a particular topic and the various subtopics; in other situations, I might have prepared materials to address only one question (of course, a book will cover multiple issues). Having both the video and written materials allows people to use whatever learning method they prefer.

Of course, if someone has a question that I have not addressed, or if they need more specific assistance, they can send an email or call to set up a consultation. If the matter is one that has general applicability, I may simply make up a new video, send the person making the inquiry a copy, and add the video to my library. (I recently did that when someone asked me what state they should use to form a nonprofit unincorporated association—see runquist .com/nonprofit-resources/nonprofit-jurisdiction/). If the matter is not one of general applicability, then the lawyer can choose to pay me to provide the necessary direction/advice, but they keep the client. Win-win for both of us!

I haven't yet figured out if there is a way to make the videos pay for themselves, but since I need to put them together first, I expect that by the time they are done, someone will be able to help me make them available and perhaps even make money. But my principal reason for putting them together is to pass on information to other lawyers who also want to move from representing the dark side.

There is another area I have thought to develop further. Based on conversations with others, this might even be more popular than the videos: I have developed a number of forms for use in forming, operating, merging, and dissolving nonprofits. I have programmed them using HotDocs, so that the options are built into the forms, and information needs to be input only once to populate the various forms. Some of the forms are relatively straightforward; some are pretty complex. One that is likely to be popular, my nonprofit bylaws form, has over 400 built-in variables. Depending on how one answers the questions, variables are added or deleted. For example, some variables are asked only if the organization is a membership corporation; others become live if the organization will not have members. There are different variables for public benefit, mutual benefit, and religious corporations. This allows the user to make sure that there are no inconsistent provisions.

Once I generate the form, I go through the resulting bylaws to make any other additional modifications that are desired but have not been built into the form itself. This is a much better option than starting with a document drafted for a different client and then making modifications.

Although my forms to date mostly follow California law, I did start to modify some of them to comply with other state laws as well. My biggest concern is that I developed the forms to the point where they are very useful, but I have never spent the time cleaning them up so that someone who is unfamiliar with the forms and the law could rely upon them to be in final form. As a result, I will have to devote a significant amount of time to the project if I decide to develop these to the point where they could be sold commercially.

That being said, after I finish the basic videos, I may try to combine a video with a form as well. Some would be very state specific (for example, requirements for the articles of incorporation will vary from state to state and would require users to select the state form they wish to use). I am currently thinking to start by developing articles and bylaws that conform to one or more versions of the Model Nonprofit Corporation Law (developed and published by the ABA Business Law Section). Although not every state has adopted a version of this law, a number have, and even those that have not used the Model Law as the basis for the law they adopt are likely to have at least considered the Model Laws. Even if the laws differ, many of the concepts will be the same or similar. I already know lawyers who would like my forms; however, to date I have not decided if I want to spend the time to finalize and market them.

One question that always comes up is who will/should my market be. I really would prefer to offer my services, information, and particularly forms to other lawyers and not to the end user for several reasons. By making the information and forms available to other lawyers, I am not actually responsible for the legal advice being given to the client. With clients I represent, I make sure that I understand their particular concerns and objectives so that when I give advice and draft documents, it is a one-on-one process where I can be sure that the advice I am giving is correct *for their particular situation.*

I am concerned that if nonlawyers take it upon themselves to use my forms without understanding the reasons to make one choice rather than another, the resulting documents may not be appropriate to achieve their desired goals. And I do not wish to compete with the existing services that assist individuals to draft their own documents. I have had to redo the articles and bylaws for too many nonprofit corporations formed using such a service to be convinced that this is a good idea.

Which brings me back to the question of referrals. Because I don't have enough to do, I have started to actually collect a list of lawyers (and some CPAs) who regularly represent nonprofit organizations. I plan to make the list available, broken down by state, on my website so that people will have a place to look when they need help.

Once I get all of this done, I have thought that one more fun project would be to put all of my reference materials into the form of a "charitypedia" to which anyone on my referral list could add topics and edit existing items. If enough lawyers were to participate, it could become the go-to repository for nonprofit law.

In my spare time I will play with my dogs.

And you? What do you want to pass on to the next generation?

# 13

## Pro Bono Work after Retiring

*by Joan M. Burda*

For many lawyers, retirement is viewed as a time of relaxation and heavy sighs of relief because the stress and strain of practicing law is behind them. Then reality sets in, and the idea of not being a lawyer becomes the source of stress and strain.

We spend considerable time learning and honing our skills as lawyers. For 30, 40, or 50 years the law is an integral part of our lives. Our personal identity is often merely an extension of our professional identity. When asked what we do, we respond, "I'm a lawyer." Being a lawyer is not only **what** we do but **who** we are. Take that away and many of us experience an identity crisis. Perhaps that is why we hold on to the practice of law, refusing to leave our firms and relinquish the one thing that embodies us.

But take heart—there is an alternative. Pro bono work, which many lawyers avoid during their career, can provide the segue into retirement that we need. Every lawyer knows there is a significant percentage of the population that cannot afford a lawyer. Pro se representation in courts is steadily rising. An increasing number of jurisdictions are seeking ways to address these unmet needs.

And most of us realize that being a licensed lawyer is an honor that carries with it a profound sense of duty to the rule of law and equal justice under the law.

# Emeritus Lawyer Programs

Forty-three states and the District of Columbia have emeritus pro bono programs. The rules in each state vary. The American Bar Association Commission on Aging has a resource page on these programs, ABA Emeritus Pro Bono (https://www.americanbar.org/groups/law_aging/resources/emeritus_pro_bono/).

Seven states—Indiana, Louisiana, Michigan, Missouri, Nebraska, Oklahoma, and Rhode Island—are the outliers. However, lawyers in those states may be able to convince the state bar and the state's supreme court to adopt the program.

These emeritus programs may be comparable to the long-standing program known as Senior Core of Retired Executives (SCORE). Participants in that program provide free advice and counsel to entrepreneurs and businesses. They utilize their experience and business savvy to help others achieve success. It is a brain trust that is, too often, underutilized.

Lawyers can do something similar. The years of training and practice provide us with a unique insight into the practice of law, litigation, transactional practice, and client relations. Further, we have developed our law practices and understand how to run a business. Young lawyers and solo and small firms are in dire need of all of these skills. Even some of the larger firms could be well served by calling on retired lawyers for counsel and advice. After all, retired lawyers no longer have a dog in the fight and are best positioned to provide honest responses to questions. We no longer need to worry about the firm politics or whether our positions will insult the firm partners.

Granted, some lawyers may market their consulting services to firms. If we can get paid, all the better. Still, providing pro bono consulting services allows us to make the profession better.

# Legal Aid Programs

But lawyers and law firms are not the only potential beneficiaries of our years of experience. Legal aid offices around the country are overloaded with calls from prospective clients—calls they cannot take and people they cannot represent.

The type of cases handled by legal aid programs varies by state and by office. Federal law also places restrictions on the kinds of legal services legal aid offices can provide. Operating independently of legal aid, private pro bono lawyers can provide services to populations that legal aid is prohibited from helping.

The Legal Services Corporation (LSC) Act (42 U.S.C. § 2996 *et seq.*) provides that LSC-funded programs cannot use either LSC or private funds for certain activities. These are some examples of some of the prohibitions:

- Representing people who are not U.S. citizens with limited exceptions such as lawful permanent residents, H2A agricultural workers, H2B forestry workers, and victims of battering, extreme cruelty, sexual assault, or trafficking.
- Criminal cases, except for cases in Indian tribal courts.
- Abortion-related litigation of any kind.
- Proceedings involving desegregation of public schools, military service, or assisted suicide.
- Habeas corpus actions challenging criminal convictions against officers of the court or law enforcement officers.
- Class actions.
- Representing prisoners.

- Representing people who are being evicted from public housing because they face criminal charges of selling or distributing illegal drugs.
- Most activities involving welfare reform.

Many people require assistance in all of these areas and, while people with adequate resources can have redress of their grievances, the poor cannot.

Of course, there are myriad ways to assist legal aid in areas of law that are not prohibited. Most legal aid offices conduct some type of community legal assistance clinic. These are staffed with volunteer lawyers. In many cases, these are "advice only" clinics and the lawyers are not expected to accept cases from the clients who come to the clinic. Lawyers are not prohibited from accepting cases that strike their fancy; however, there are no expectations that they do so.

Volunteering to provide services to these groups, independent of legal aid, is another opportunity for lawyers to use their skills and training to help people who have nowhere else to go.

Given the LSC restrictions, it may be necessary to find a way to provide pro bono services without running afoul of those prohibitions. That allows us to be creative, something we may have had limited opportunity to explore during our careers.

# Hospice Organizations

Hospice organizations present another untapped area of potential pro bono possibilities. Introduced in the United States in the 1970s, hospice care is increasing, and many companies offer free legal assistance to low- and middle-income hospice patients. The Hospice Foundation of America, the National Association for Home Care and Hospice, and the National Hospice and Palliative Care Organization are a few of the national organizations providing information on hospice care in the United States.

Hospice of the Western Reserve (HWR) in Northeast Ohio is one of them. This organization began operating in April 1984. They recruit volunteer lawyers, many of them in active practice, to provide basic legal assistance to hospice patients. Lawyers are called upon to draft simple wills and powers of attorney, notarize documents, and explain a patient's options concerning property and family. In some cases, the lawyers participate in panels explaining to other volunteers what they do. There are also opportunities to present brief seminars in which the lawyers explain what the different types of forms are and why they are necessary.

Volunteering in this type of program does not need to be a solitary endeavor. Get the names of other volunteer lawyers and seek their advice on best practices. When possible, shadow another volunteer. It helps to get a feel for the situation. For many lawyers, providing these types of services, in varying circumstances, is outside their normal forum. This is especially true for lawyers whose background is in law firms that never went to a client's home or visited a client in a hospital or long-term care facility.

In 2016, HWR applied to be and was approved as an entity through which lawyers could receive continuing legal education credit for their pro bono work. HWR is the only non–legal aid entity included on the list of approved pro bono programs in Ohio.

The time involved in volunteering for this type of program is minimal. However, often the need is immediate because of the type of person in hospice. The lawyer has sole authority to determine a patient's competency to execute documents. And, yes, there are times when the lawyer must tell the family it's too late because the patient is no longer able to make his or her wishes known. And legal assistance is very basic. Patients who express a desire for trusts or more extensive planning are directed to contact the local bar association.

At the same time, there are circumstances when the lawyer is called upon to referee disputes within a dysfunctional family, like the grandchild who wants to know what she will get. That also gives a certain amount of satisfaction in explaining why the person's priorities are misplaced. In any event, these are not long-term client matters. Assisting hospice patients falls into the "one and done" category.

Participating in this type of program imparts a level of professional satisfaction. Volunteer lawyers provide hospice patients, and their families, with peace of mind because their questions are being answered.

## Nonprofit Organizations

Pro bono work can also include assisting nonprofit organizations by serving on a board of directors or providing legal assistance in drafting corporate papers that need to be filed with the state. Most nonprofits have limited funds, and paying for a lawyer is usually not included in the budget. However, assisting a nonprofit in applying for a grant or seeking 501(c)(3) status with the Internal Revenue Service is a rewarding way to support a good cause and keep your hand in the game.

One type of volunteer opportunity is through a bar association's Volunteer Lawyers for the Arts. Many local and state bar associations have these committees. These volunteer lawyers assist artists, writers, poets, musicians, etc., in resolving legal problems or teaching them how to avoid problems in the first place.

## Court Pro Se Programs

A growing number of courts are initiating pro se programs to accommodate the increasing number of pro se litigants who are filing or defending cases. Most of these people cannot afford to hire a lawyer and have no choice but to proceed on their own.

Too many members of the bar believe that pro se litigants, and those who come to legal aid advice-only clinics, could afford a lawyer, if they wanted. These lawyers believe the people just don't want to hire a lawyer. For the most part, this is a fallacy.

Consider a person whose sole source of income is Supplemental Security Income. That usually amounts to $750 a month, from which the person must pay rent, utilities, grocery bills, and other expenses. People in that situation cannot afford to hire a lawyer. A volunteer lawyer is in a position to ensure that person has as much access to the judicial system as someone able to hire a cadre of lawyers.

Many pro se litigants are defending themselves against lawsuits filed by lawyers. They are at a distinct disadvantage in a courtroom. A volunteer lawyer, even one with little courtroom experience, can help level the playing field.

# Limited Scope Representation

Short of going to court, a volunteer lawyer can provide legal assistance in the form of bundled or limited scope representation. This allows the lawyer to draft documents for the client to sign, provide guidance on how to proceed in court, and answer questions that crop up during the process.

Providing these services to otherwise unrepresented individuals can serve the interests of justice and assist the court in maintaining an orderly progression of cases. As everyone knows, pro se litigants are not, for the most part, knowledgeable about court rules and procedures.

It may be possible to offer this as a pro bono option to your former law firm. Giving you an office to provide limited scope representation allows the firm to claim pro bono services and you an opportunity to put your skills and training to good use. Further, you will serve as an example to younger lawyers that practicing law can serve a higher good and is more than billable hours.

# Bar Association Opportunities

Volunteer opportunities after retirement that are short of providing actual hands-on legal assistance may also be available. Your city, county, or state bar association may have programs offering pro bono services to low- or middle-income people in your area. Volunteering to mentor younger lawyers is another way to serve. Most law schools provide some clinical experience, but there are not enough slots for all the students who want to participate. This results in young lawyers graduating with limited experience representing clients. We all know that representing a client is more than just preparing documents. There is an art to attorney-client relationships that is too often misunderstood by both parties. Younger lawyers are at a distinct disadvantage because of their limited experience. As an experienced lawyer, you have an opportunity to provide a safe sounding board for those lawyers who want to learn but don't know whom to ask.

It may require you to initiate a program with the bar association. Or the bar may sponsor or cosponsor community clinics in which you can participate. It falls into the category of mentor/monitor. We can all remember the discomfort we felt when we began practicing law and were unsure of the next step. You can be the person to provide that next step and save the next generation of lawyers from foundering.

# American Bar Association Programs

The American Bar Association has programs that require volunteers, including the Central European and Eurasian Law Initiative (CEELI). The opportunities in this program are much different than volunteering with your local legal aid office.

The opportunities CEELI presents involve parts of the world where the idea of the rule of law is new and untested. Some of the countries participating in the program are former Soviet satellites.

Other opportunities exist in Africa, Asia, Latin America, and the Middle East. You can volunteer your skills, training, and experience to help another country initiate a judicial system that is fair and impartial or assist local lawyers in developing training programs that allow them to hone their skills.

For overseas participants who serve 90 days or longer, there is a living and housing allowance, transportation, medical evacuation coverage, business expenses, limited reimbursement for foreign language study, and ABA dues waivers. There are also shorter assignments that provide lodging, meals, transportation, and business expenses.

The world has long seen the United States as a country that values justice. The CEELI program gives you an opportunity to confirm this perception. Any way you put it, this will take you out of your comfort zone but give you an immense feeling of satisfaction and accomplishment.

## Malpractice Insurance

Volunteering to provide pro bono legal services may require the lawyer to maintain malpractice insurance. Legal aid may cover the lawyers under the program's malpractice policy. In any event, it is important to check. Get a copy of the policy and have written verification from the issuer that you are covered. Even in retirement, we need to remember to "get it in writing."

## Varying Practice Areas

Pro bono programs offer lawyers an opportunity to engage in different areas of law. Sometimes, those areas are far removed from the type of law the lawyer practiced. That should not be a deterrent. We are lawyers, and few of us graduated from law school knowing what we were doing. We are accustomed to on-the-job training. And learning a new area of law helps us maintain our intellectual curiosity.

The types of problems you may encounter in pro bono work include divorce, custody, child support, visitation, guardianship, criminal record expungement, paternity, bankruptcy, homelessness, landlord/tenant, foreclosure proceedings, misdemeanor criminal charges, Social Security disability claims, Supplemental Security Income applications, veterans' benefits and other types of public benefits, nonprofit, artists, copyright, and the list goes on.

Don't let the variety frighten you. It's a challenge that any experienced lawyer is more than capable of handling.

# Wrapping Up

Retiring from the practice of law does not mean you must give up being a lawyer. The training and skills you developed over the years continue to be a valuable commodity. Not having to worry about billable hours, rainmaking, and the other requirements of an active practice releases you to do what you do best—practice law and represent client interests. The issues and the clients may not be the same, but the need is ever present. And you are in a unique position to provide a valuable service. After all, lawyers can do things other people cannot: give legal advice, advocate for those who cannot do so for themselves, and help provide people with a solution to what may seem to them to be insurmountable problems.

There may also be a need to provide something other than legal assistance. Sometimes it means figuring out that what a client needs is housing and helping them find it. Or learning how to navigate the local veterans' hospital to get needed medical care. As lawyers, we do many things and wear many different hats. Practicing law is just one of them. But it opens a gateway to resolving problems.

Think about it.

# Part V

# There's More to Life Than Practicing Law

Lawyers had lives before they were ever admitted to practice, and far too many of them became just too caught up in the practice of law to enjoy their lives to the fullest. Second acts are all about using free time to pursue different directions, sometimes putting lessons learned and talents developed in the practice to good use, and sometimes just exploring different avenues. It's all good.

**Chapter 14**

Finding Fulfillment by Serving on a Volunteer Board of Directors
*Jeffrey Allen*

**Chapter 15**

Confessions of a Recovering Divorce Lawyer
*Jimmy Verner*

**Chapter 16**

Teaching before and during Retirement
*Joan M. Burda*

**Chapter 17**

RVing for Retiring Lawyers: Driving toward the Future
*Vicki Levy Eskin*

**Chapter 18**

Retiring at My Own Speed
*Wendy Cole Lascher*

**Chapter 19**

From Courtroom to Cockpit
*Capt. David R. Hammer*

**Chapter 20**

Picture This: The Journey to My Second Act
*Victoria L. Herring*

# 14

# Finding Fulfillment by Serving on a Volunteer Board of Directors

*by Jeffrey Allen*

Throughout my adult life, I have always believed that I had an obligation to give back to the community. During my career as a lawyer, I have respected that belief by doing a lot of community service. Much of that service related to the administration of various entities, ranging from bar associations to Rotary to youth and adult sports organizations to a variety of public service organizations. In many of those organizations I ended up serving as a member of the board of directors. I have found it challenging, interesting, and stimulating to work on the board of directors of these various organizations. Now that I have moved to semiretirement, I look forward to even more opportunities to work as a volunteer with such organizations, because I enjoy the work and because it helps keep me busy and involved in positive and productive activities.

Serving on a volunteer board differs in some respects from serving as a compensated member of the board of directors. In other ways you will find it very similar. It differs in that you do not receive compensation for your time. It differs in that you do not have as much regulation as you do, for example, in a publicly traded corporation. It differs in that you usually can become involved at the higher levels of administration of local charitable organizations (or local chapters of national organizations) without having the connections that you would need to become involved in the administration of national charitable organizations or in for-profit compensated board positions.

While you could also say that it differs in that you do not have large investors to deal with or answer to, that would probably cause a misleading conclusion. A great many volunteer boards have to deal with serious issues and strong demands from those who have invested their time in the organization and those with a vested interest in its activities. For example, as a member of the board of directors of a youth sports organization, you would, more likely than not, end up dealing with complaints by parents of youth players who deem themselves aggrieved because their offspring has not succeeded as well as others or had as much time to play as others, as well as having to address issues and set policies that deal with such things as gender identification, prevention of child abuse, prevention of sexual abuse, and discrimination. Those issues and the people involved with them can be as intense in their feelings and actions as major investors and stockholders in a publicly traded corporation—sometimes even more so, as these are strong emotional issues, not simply financial issues.

Whether you serve as a director of a charitable or not-for-profit organization or as a director of a for-profit, you have fiduciary obligations to the stakeholders (whether you call them members or shareholders or something else). Those fiduciary duties do not change based on whether you receive monetary compensation for your services. While attending law school certainly does not present the only way to learn about fiduciary obligations, having attended law school will predispose you to understand what they mean, how they operate, and how they play into the work of the board of directors.

On the other hand, you can likely find considerable satisfaction in solving some of the problems that the organization faces and in improving its operation. From my perspective a lawyer is optimally situated to serve on boards of directors of such organizations. In most cases, a lawyer will have training in and knowledge of the obligations of the board of directors and its membership that someone without legal training is less likely to possess. Even if the lawyer did not practice in that area or even take corporations in law school, lawyers have training that will enable them to review applicable law, rules, and regulations and quickly acquire the knowledge required to work effectively in the organization. In fact, my experience has been that a lawyer serving on a volunteer board more often than not ends up answering procedural and substantive law questions that may impact the organization. Even if that does not come up, lawyers tend to have a logical business-oriented perception of problems and how to deal with them. As a result of one or both of those things, I have found it fairly common that others on the board start perceiving the lawyer as a leader within the board's internal organization and operation.

Once perceived as a leader, the lawyer may find that the door to election as an officer opens fairly quickly. While serving as an officer of an entity presents some differences to serving only as a member of the board of directors, I will discuss both in this chapter, as I consider serving as an officer to be effectively an extension of serving as a member of the board of directors.

Because this chapter focuses on volunteer service as a member of the board of directors of an organization, I will also focus on not-for-profit or charitable organizations, as they present many of the opportunities for such involvement by interested people of all ages and many and varied backgrounds. For convenience, I have set up seven general classifications of such organizations. That is not to suggest that all such organizations fit into one of these classifications; in fact, many don't. My purpose in using these classifications is to start you thinking about areas in which you might find it interesting to volunteer.

1.   **Youth and adult sports organizations.** Baseball, soccer, football, basketball, volleyball, etc., organizations for both youth and adults require organization and administration. Generally, somewhere along the line, someone put a corporation together for administrative purposes. Many of these organizations exist with distinctions sometimes based on geography, age, gender, and level of play. Sometimes, organizations have state and national affiliations, so even more opportunities exist for those who become involved at the local level to elevate to state, regional, and even national involvement. I will give you a brief example of how that can work out of my personal experience. Throughout my career as a lawyer, I worked in youth soccer as a coach, a referee, and ultimately an administrator. I started as a director of a club within a citywide league. I ended up moving from the club to the league board to the district board (several cities in two counties) to the state board to the regional board (several states). While I did not serve on the national board, I did become actively involved at the national level. While working in youth soccer, I also got involved in adult soccer in respect to both the player and the administration of the referee program, moving up the ranks from one board to another and serving on the state boards of directors for the adult soccer program and for the referee administration. Ultimately, I focused on indoor soccer and became a member of the board of directors of the U.S. Futsal Federation (now called U.S. Futsal). After about ten years on the board as a member and an officer (CFO), I currently serve as the chairman of the board. Virtually every organized youth and adult sports program needs people to get involved and help administer the program fairly and even-handedly.

2.   **Community service organizations.** Many professionals join community service organizations for a variety of reasons. While historically many lawyers were advised to join such

organizations to get themselves known and, hopefully, generate business, my experience and conversations with other lawyers suggest that does not work very well these days (if ever it did) and I will suggest that it is a wrong-headed way to look at participation in such organizations. Join an organization because it does something you think worth doing. Participate because it provides an organized way for you to help others and because it gives you personal satisfaction. As you participate more, become a leader as you have the ability to do so (in no small part due to your legal training and experience). Examples of such organizations include, without limitation, Rotary, Elks, Moose, Masons, Big Brothers Big Sisters, Humane Society, United Way, Red Cross, Habitat for Humanity, NAACP, ACLU, Trayvon Martin Foundation, Incite! (Women of Color Against Violence), Latino Community Services, Inc., MALDEF, The League of United Latin American Citizens, GLBT National Help Center, Family Equality Council, and Human Rights Campaign. Please note that I do not intend this as an all-inclusive list. It represents a small fraction of the community service organizations available for you to join as a member, as a volunteer, and perhaps, if you have the interest, ultimately as a member of the board of directors or even as an officer of the organization. Find one and start the ball rolling by joining. The more you put into such efforts, the more you will likely get out of them in terms of personal satisfaction, whether or not you ultimately become a member of the board of directors. Note that I have included in this section some organizations that have highly political issues at their core. The line between politics and community service can often become very blurry. For example, would you classify becoming involved with KIND (Kids in Need of Defense), an organization that provides legal assistance to minors dealing with immigration issues and facing deportation without any legal representation, as a community service activity, making a political statement, or both?

3.  **Providing/fundraising organizations.** In this category, I include organizations that collect and distribute resources for those who need food, clothing, shelter, etc., and/or use the collection and reselling of goods to raise funds for various medical causes, such as heart disease or cancer research.

4.  **School or alumni organizations.** Most colleges, universities, and professional schools (including law schools) have active alumni associations that coordinate with the school in raising funds for the school as well as the operation of the association. Alumni associations present one of the most common of those organizations. Alumni associations have social functions but exist primarily to facilitate fundraising operations for the school.

5.  **Political organizations.** While nobody seems to know who first said "politics gives rise to strange bedfellows" (some credit Charles Dudley Warner), the general consensus is that it derives from a line in Shakespeare's *The Tempest*. Without regard to its derivation, the fact remains that innumerable local political organizations come into and disappear from existence every year. If you find a cause that interests you and an organization forms to address it, consider joining and putting some time into it. Who knows, you might end up changing something or helping to solve a problem. If the organization does not exist, you might consider starting one (incidentally, there is no better way to assure yourself of a position on the board of directors of an organization than involving yourself or taking the lead in the creation of that organization).

6.  **Social organizations.** While almost every organization has a social element to it and involvement in the activities of an organization at most levels gives rise to social interactions, some organizations exist for primarily, if not purely,

social reasons—book clubs, neighborhood organizations, knitting clubs, etc.

7.  **Religious organizations.** I do not refer to the religious organization itself. Religious organizations generally have their own internal organizational structure. I refer to organizations created by members of a religious group loosely banded together to provide community service (often for members of that religious group, but sometimes not so limited). If you actively belong to a particular religious group, this may be a particularly good option for you. According to GuideStar (https://www.guidestar.org/NonprofitDirectory.aspx?cat=8), tens of thousands of such organizations currently exist in the United States.

It would prove unusual to start out with an organization as a member of its board of directors, but such things do not lack precedent. Over the years I have seen that occur on multiple occasions and can recall at least one where I had no prior involvement with one particular community service organization but was approached by a current member of its board to allow myself to become appointed as a member of the board of directors. I agreed to do that, because I both respected the individual who had approached me and thought well of the organization. Shortly after that I became a director of the organization and, two years later, chairman of its board of directors.

Clearly, you have many opportunities available to you in this area. While serving in such a capacity can prove interesting and rewarding, do not lightly undertake it. Give considerable thought to the decision as to both your willingness and ability to devote proper time and attention to it and the risks it can pose to you. Do your due diligence before you agree. Here are some things you should think about in that regard.

1.  Before you get involved with an organization (especially if you have not previously worked with it), learn as much as

you can about it and how it operates. You should probably talk to a member of the board of directors (ideally a lawyer) to find out how the organization operates and how it addresses legal questions that may arise.

2.  Be sure you are comfortable with the type, nature, and scope of the activities regularly engaged in by the entity. You want to have a reasonable comfort level with what the organization will likely do while you are affiliated with it.

3.  If you still practice law, what likelihood is there that your involvement will create a conflict of interest respecting your current or potential clients? You should also consider the likelihood of a conflict arising in connection with former clients.

4.  Does the organization have directors' and officers' liability coverage? If so, satisfy yourself that the coverage is adequate and that you trust the carrier. If not, you expose your personal assets to risk. I have made it a point to never serve on the board of directors of any organization that did not provide adequate directors' and officers' liability coverage. Some states have protective legislation that gives some insulation to volunteer directors in terms of liability. Those protections generally require that the director act reasonably and in good faith. That requirement often gets met by seeking a legal opinion about a particular action. Be careful that because you are a lawyer, you do not become everyone else's protection without having your own. I do not recommend that you consider such a provision as satisfying the requirement of liability insurance, if for no other reason than that the liability insurance should include defense costs and the protective legislation does not.

5.  Related to the issue raised in the preceding paragraph, does the organization make use of outside legal counsel? If so, are you comfortable with that counsel? Regardless, be forewarned that I have observed a marked tendency to

simply ask the lawyer/director because that person happens to be in the room. When that happens, do not expect to send a bill to the organization for your time and opinion; they will most likely expect you to just provide that information as part of the package (a fringe benefit to having a lawyer as a director). Similarly, particularly in smaller organizations, you may be asked to do legal work for the organization (with or without compensation). Remember that whenever you do legal work or provide legal advice, you put your malpractice insurance on the line (as well as your personal assets if you do not have malpractice insurance or it does not cover the risk). If you do provide legal services to the organization, you should make it clear in a written representation agreement what is a director activity and what is a legal activity that you will bill for. Note also that some malpractice insurance coverage limits or excludes liability for representation of corporations in which the lawyer serves as a director or officer.

6.   You should also be aware that when organizations do fundraising, the first thing fundraisers often discuss is the need to have all the members of the board of directors make a contribution, as it is difficult to get an outsider to donate if the insiders won't or don't. That is not to say they will expect you to become a major donor, but they will likely expect you to make a donation.

# 15

## Confessions of a Recovering Divorce Lawyer

*by Jimmy Verner*

Back in the day, in 1974, I had finished my undergrad coursework at the University of Utah in Salt Lake City. Having majored in political science, I figured I was cut out to be a bartender. I got a job at D.B. Cooper's, of hijacking fame, where the FBI actually checked us out. We were legit—it was just a name, so there were no issues.

Before long, the yearning to do something more with my life resurfaced. I graduated in 1975 and headed for Alabama, where my parents lived. My family was from the South, so I thought I'd check it out. My mom suggested that I begin climbing the corporate ladder. My dad suggested graduate school. Enrolling in Emory University, I received an MA in political science the following year.

In the meantime, like many in my generation, I searched for what to do next. I settled on law school. I applied for admission to several. There was no Internet, no email, and no fax machines. I wrote to the schools for applications, filled them out with a typewriter, and then mailed them back. I got accepted at two out of four and picked the University of San Diego.

**135**

Each of the applications included a section on why I wanted to be a lawyer. The answer space was limited to 250 words, so I figured it couldn't be too important. But I decided not to blow any smoke and said in various ways that I wanted to help other people. How well I've done that, and done what I could to keep myself sane in the process, is a theme of this chapter.

As any lawyer knows, law school was a bitch. Think like a lawyer! *Marbury v. Madison*! Who cares if the guy didn't have a driver's license—was he negligent? What was the actor's mens rea? You who have been there will remember.

I was interested in international law but wanted to become a trial lawyer. Not much crossover there, right? But I dove into law school. I got on the law review not from stellar grades but through a writing competition.

I parlayed my resume and desire to return to the South into a clerkship for a federal district court judge in Mississippi. My thought was that it would be a good idea to watch lawyers try cases before doing it myself. And why Mississippi? My parents lived in Memphis by then, so it was close to home, just down the river in Greenville.

Clerking remains one of the more memorable experiences of my life. I still think about it sometimes, even though I finished 37 years ago. I learned so much and came to understand how trial courts work from the other side of the bench. That perspective taught me a lot about trial work.

After my clerkship, I practiced briefly in Greenville, but things moved slowly in the Mississippi Delta. I decided to relocate to the big city of Memphis, where I was privileged to work at what is now known as Martin Tate. They were, and still are, fine lawyers. I enjoyed working there, but I still had the trial-lawyer itch. Even though it was Memphis, it was still a sleepy Southern city.

Texas beckoned. There was a banking crisis. It developed into a full-blown litigation riot by the mid-1980s. I liked commercial litigation, so I looked for and found a job in Dallas.

"Holy cow!" as they say. People, entities, and institutions were suing each other right and left in Dallas. It was a lot of fun for a while. I tried a bunch of jury trials. But the courts eventually got so clogged up that you couldn't get much done. And the bankruptcy lawyers kept putting a halt to litigation with their filings. It didn't seem fair that you could freeze a lawsuit by filing a one-page pleading! I followed a few cases into bankruptcy court. I did enough bankruptcy work to realize that it wasn't my cup of tea.

Eventually I decided commercial litigation didn't move fast enough. Especially in federal court, you would file a lawsuit and then forget it because nothing happened for a year and a half. So—God help me—I decided to jump into family law.

Back then, there were no standing orders. Once you filed for or got sued for divorce, you faced a wide-open temporary orders hearing within two weeks. You still do face a hearing if you don't work things out, but standing orders have made the process not as wild as it once was. Still, what happens at the temporary orders hearing tends to be what happens on final trial, so you have to scramble.

My commercial litigation experience served me well in family court on the property side. But there was the human side, too, especially in what we call suits affecting the parent-child relationship—in other words, custody and visitation. There are divorce lawyers who say that you see good people at their worst in divorce cases. That's true sometimes. I'd add that you see some real SOBs at their worst, too.

I learned about the cycle of domestic abuse. I learned about people who cut themselves, and I became acquainted with a variety of psychotropic drugs. But the sociopaths stood out to me. They are now called people with antisocial personality disorder. Have you ever met anyone with shark eyes? You might have met a sociopath.

There are many other troubling diagnoses in the American Psychiatric Association's Diagnostic and Statistical Manual of Mental

Disorders. FYI, the DSM is now up to its fifth edition. Back then, it was DSM-IV. We kept a well-thumbed copy in the office.

In my late 30s, I found that every month, or maybe every six weeks, I simply could not function for two or three days. I would go to work, because that was my duty, but I couldn't really do anything. After seeking medical attention, I was diagnosed with dysthymia, which means that I was depressed such that my normal mood was below everyone else's. I was astonished when the shrink told me that most people's default moods are somewhat good. Mine were not. So I began taking Paxil, then later Cymbalta. I'll leave it to the chemists to explain how these drugs work, but the net effect was that now my moods are pretty much the same as anyone else's. It was, and is, a godsend.

Contrary to some uninformed beliefs, antidepressants are not "happy pills." I have good days and blue days just like everyone else. The key here is "everyone else."

The 1990s were go-go. My partners Janet and Paul and I litigated family law cases not just in Dallas but in many other places in Texas. Janet has the ability to attract clients by the force of her personality. Paul is gregarious and easy to talk to. My strength was more bookish. I solicited speaking engagements all over Texas and spoke anywhere that would have me. It was busy but fun.

City and county bar associations are always looking for speakers, especially speakers who will get their presentations accredited for MCLE hours. If you're willing to research and write plus travel on your own dime, you will have as many speaking engagements as you want. Often, you will get a free lunch, but you have to eat *fast* because you will be up in just a moment. Eventually the other lawyers will come to know and remember you, and the referrals will come.

After a while, my do-gooder intentions hit a wall. Because I wanted to help people, I made the mistake of sometimes representing people who felt they had been mistreated by the system.

Some of them were, colloquially speaking, crazy. I believed that these people deserved representation just like anyone else. But they were not grateful if things didn't turn out to their liking. I had three grievances in successive years. They were all frivolous and dismissed, but they wore me out and burned me out.

By 2000, I had focused my practice on family law appeals. I enjoy research and writing. There's minimal client contact because the case is limited to the record. It's difficult to win any appeal, but family law appeals are more difficult than most. That's because most issues are subject to the abuse-of-discretion standard of review. I explained this to clients, but many wanted to go forward anyhow. I won some, often did not, but the clients at least got the satisfaction of having been heard.

Not long afterward, I decided to go back to grad school. I enrolled in the PhD program at the University of Texas at Dallas in 2003. I practiced law while studying part-time. Six long years later, I received my PhD in Public Policy and Political Economy. It's a political science degree heavy on the economics. I studied development economics and economic justice issues. My dissertation demonstrates empirically that raising the minimum wage causes only a tiny rise in unemployment and then only in the month of the increase.

In the meantime, I kept fooling around with child support calculations. At one time, a Texas court, within its discretion, could set child support within a range. That led to numerous court hearings over exactly what percent child support should be. The Texas legislature simplified and streamlined the calculation of child support by enacting statutes that mathematically determined, to the penny, the amount of child support to be paid by those within the guidelines, which encompass most people who are divorcing.

There aren't that many variables to consider when calculating child support in Texas. It's just a matter of deciphering the statutes and creating a series of if/then calculations based on them. One day in 2009, our associate asked why I didn't build a child support calculator and put it on the iTunes Store, which had just opened in mid-2008. ("There's an app for that!") I had some coding skills from grad school. I got a tech guy to help me with the app itself. The Texas Child Support Calculator remains one of my proudest accomplishments.

---

In my early 50s, I found that I was having frequent, involuntary micronaps. I could not drive for more than fifteen miles without having to pull over for a quick nap. I was getting up as many as twenty times per night to pee. Hello, sleep apnea!

This disease substantially affects your quality of life. Plus, it's really dangerous. Not only might you nod off while driving, but the reason you pee so much at night is that when you can't breathe, your blood pressure soars. Your body says "pee!" to relieve the blood pressure. Sleep apnea leads to strokes. If you feel like I did, go see a doc. My CPAP machine is a lifesaver.

---

I'd had a thought that I would retire from practicing law and teach. I could teach various topics within the common law legal system, especially as Americanized, and econometrics. Unfortunately, universities look for young people to appoint as assistant professors—by then I was in my late 50s—and being an adjunct pays crap. My wife is a physician. There were jobs for both of us overseas. We thought about working abroad for a six-, 12-, or 24-month term, but we have family here in Dallas plus pets we didn't want to leave. My wife now accuses me of getting my PhD "apparently just for kicks."

So we rocked along—me becoming more and more disillusioned with the practice of family law—until 2015. My wife had gone on some medical mission trips and encouraged me to go with her to attend Unite for Sight's Global Health & Innovation Conference. Unite for Sight is a nonprofit that works to save and improve eyesight around the world. Each year, it sponsors the Global Health & Innovation Conference. The conference has an overall medical theme but covers other areas, too.

I went with her, and it was a blast. The conference included pitches by startups. The pitches were both for practice in obtaining grants and for small amounts of funding awarded at the conference itself. I learned about ingenious ways to deliver health-care services in third-world countries, cost-effective techniques for purifying water, microfinancing facilitated by cellphone, and much more. I was impressed and encouraged by all these young people trying to change the world for the better.

One topic that interested me from a legal point of view is the concept of a social enterprise. We all know from corporations law class that the primary duty of corporate officers and directors is to enhance shareholder value. If they fail in that endeavor, they can be forced out and even sued. In the social enterprise, the board must give equal consideration to how corporate actions would affect the environment, economy, workplace, public health, and other areas of civic concern. The social enterprise is for profit, but directors are shielded from accusations that they breached their fiduciary duty to shareholders by taking into account social interests when making decisions for the corporation.

The conference inspired me so much that I began studying startup law, nonprofits, social enterprises, and benefit corporations. I built out a website, did a couple of lectures for entrepreneurs at an incubator, and gave a guest lecture at a nearby college. The legal work didn't come. Even though I offered my services dirt cheap, startups are cash-strapped. But then I discovered how to work mostly online.

When I built my child support calculator, I found my tech help through a website called freelancer (freelancer.com). You would post a project, receive bids, pick one, escrow the money, and the freelancer would get the job done. The bids I received on freelancer were far less than those from U.S.-based companies for the same work. In fact, I inadvertently learned that one California-based company was offering to build apps for the iTunes Store for $25,000. Their business model was to outsource overseas rather than do the work themselves. Pretty sneaky. In any event, through freelancer, I worked with people from Eastern and Western Europe, East Asia, and Central America.

Freelancer is geared toward tech work, but I looked for jobs on freelancer that required legal skills anyway. No bites. Then I found out about a similar web-based market called Thumbtack (thumbtack.com). I picked up a few jobs setting up LLCs or corporations and drafting contracts. My wife began calling me a "Thumbtack lawyer."

She should have waited to label me. I finally found a web-based market called Upwork (upwork.com). Upwork lists all kinds of jobs—tech, research, writing, PR, and so forth, including legal work. I quickly picked up quite a bit of work online from Upwork.

Who knew that organizational and transactional law could be so much less stressful than litigation and so much more rewarding? That's not to say that transactional law cannot be stressful, too, but for me it does not compare with litigation, especially in family court.

To keep a successful law practice running, you must make rain. I faltered after the Unite for Sight conference, and it showed in my family law practice. But I didn't care because I was making decent money helping the youngsters and idealists—and sleeping at night. If you do family law work, and you care about your clients and especially the kiddos, you lose a lot of sleep. I can't imagine what it's like for the social workers.

And that brings me to today. Most of my work now consists of advising entrepreneurs and activists online about the best formats for what they have in mind and setting them up organizationally. Of course, there was a learning curve involved, which continues to this day. That's why they call it law "practice." But I enjoy learning new things.

I'm 64 years old at this writing. I'm certainly not rich, but I am financially secure. (Here's a tip: Take your Social Security now before Congress guts it!) I work almost exclusively out of my house and rarely go to court. I'm "on the bench" for my law firm and sometimes get called into the game. A little bit of litigation I will do, but not protracted trials. With some notable and admirable exceptions, trial lawyers are young lawyers because trial practice eats up your life if you dive into it. And if you are not careful, it can eat up your soul, at least in divorce court.

My professional career is not over yet, not by a long shot. What with the inhumane separation of children from their parents at the southern border—when the parents are seeking asylum—I've volunteered to donate legal services even though I know very little immigration law. I've begun studying and attended an excellent seminar for volunteers hosted by Haynes & Boone in Dallas. I have not been called yet because there are so many expert volunteers and my Spanish isn't that good.

I'm disappointed that I can't help right now, but I don't mind too much because the situation tells me that my fellow lawyers are overwhelmingly responding to the call to help people. And in the end, isn't that what being a lawyer is all about? I thought so when I applied to law school, and I still think so now. Color me naive or a fool, but I'm more content now than I have been in a long time.

# 16

# Teaching before and during Retirement

*by Joan M. Burda*

It's often said, "Never give a lawyer a microphone. They can talk forever to anyone about anything." That's not a bad way to look at teaching as a practice option. Whether starting while still practicing or after retiring from practice, lawyers can often find teaching opportunities at law schools, colleges, universities, and community colleges.

Adjunct professors are ubiquitous on campuses around the country. These people are teaching classes to students of all levels.

## You Won't Get Rich

Schools are notorious for paying adjunct faculty abysmal amounts. Compensation starts around $2,250 and increases depending on caseload, the institution, and what you can negotiate. On that point, be aware, there may be very little wiggle room. Still, it is a viable alternative to playing golf every day. And you will be providing a vital service to the students.

# Law School

Most law schools use adjuncts to supplement the full-time faculty. Most adjuncts teach established classes. However, there are opportunities to review the existing curriculum and propose a class that is not being offered.

Law schools also have clinics that allow students to obtain experience representing clients in court. For example, in 2011, students at Case Western Reserve University School of Law (where I am an adjunct) won a $1.1-million verdict in a home repair and financing scheme. They filed the case in state court. In 2018, law students represented a prison inmate in federal court in a case involving religious rights. Lawyers worked with the students in the Milton A. Kramer Law Clinic Center.

Students in law school clinics around the country are representing clients who cannot afford legal counsel. In some states, the state legislatures are unhappy with the success of many of these student-filed lawsuits—so much so that they react by defunding the clinics or passing laws that prohibit students from filing court cases.

Experienced lawyers are in a good position to provide students with real-world insight into how law is practiced. This includes teaching students how to communicate with clients, opposing counsel, judges, and clerks. Tenured law professors can be some of the brightest people in town. However, most of them do not practice law on a regular basis. There is a big difference between teaching theory and understanding how to put theory into practice. That is where you can come in.

In addition to clinical practice, law schools hire adjuncts to teach core courses: family law, wills and trusts, criminal law, criminal procedure, etc. A lawyer who has practiced in these areas can give students more than what is in the hornbooks. And those books, by the way, are extraordinarily expensive. An adjunct can work around having students buy an expensive textbook, opting instead for materials that include caselaw, law review articles, and

CLE materials. Students may be given an opportunity to respond to actual client issues within the safe confines of a classroom. They may not be representing actual clients but can learn how to draft documents (contracts, wills, trusts, pleadings, discovery), prepare letters, investigate cases, and come up with solutions that may not fit neatly into the theoretical parameters that they are accustomed to with other professors.

Students need drafting experience because too many law students (myself included) graduate without knowing how to do basic tasks. And students are excited about the prospect of learning an actual skill they can put to work in their first job.

You are in a position to show how the various areas of law intersect with each other—that rather than being discrete legal topics, many are intertwined, and that common sense as well as an understanding of the legal issues is required. Family law can include issues involving wills and trusts, contracts, torts, and civil procedure. We know that law is not practiced in a vacuum. With your guidance, the students will become aware of it as well.

Law school teaches students to find, read, and analyze the law. Adjuncts can teach students how to put it all together into a comprehensible format so they understand how the law does, and sometimes does not, work. It is also an opportunity to introduce students to changes in the law. Some areas of law are in a state of rapid change. That may mean updating the syllabus weekly to respond to court decisions. Students hate that kind of uncertainty, but it is a valid learning experience. It also shows them that it is possible for the practice of law to be creative.

Teaching at the law school level can be exciting and challenging. These are bright people, and they won't let you rest on your laurels. You will need to step up your game. That includes preparing for each class. A three-hour class that meets twice a week may require 20 hours of prep work. Plus, don't forget the exams and grading—by far the worst part of teaching. And grades matter to these students. On the bright side, being an adjunct means no faculty meetings, little exposure to school politics, and no requirement to "publish or perish."

In addition to serving as an adjunct and teaching classes, another alternative is to sign up with a law school's bar prep program. Many schools have introduced these programs to assist students in preparing to take the bar examination. The programs vary by school and can be a standalone class for which the students receive credit or an informal program where students are told to "study hard."

The more formal programs can be intensive for the students and the adjuncts hired to assist them. The program at Cleveland State University's Cleveland-Marshall College of Law assigns 15 to 17 students to each adjunct facilitator. Throughout the semester, students write essay answers to bar exam questions and submit them to the adjunct for grading. Twice a semester the adjunct meets individually with the assigned students and reviews their work.

The class can be labor intensive, especially regarding the grading. The students write two to three essays, and all need to be graded. However, the major reward is watching the students improve as the semester progresses. And you quickly figure out who will be successful and who will not. Some students pour heart and soul into the class, others do not. And when the bar results come out, there is a sense of satisfaction in seeing the students you worked with on the bar passage list.

# Colleges, Universities, and Community Colleges

Colleges, universities, and community colleges present different challenges. However, all three types of institutions offer law-related classes. Having licensed lawyers, with experience in specific areas, improves the quality of the class. Students are introduced to the legal issues they may face and this, in turn, prepares them for their careers. There are law-related issues in business, sociology, psychology, health services, technology, intellectual property rights, creative writing, education, and sports curricula.

As with law schools, the pay is not great, but it allows you to work with students, most of whom will be much younger, and help them understand how the law can affect their prospective professions.

You may be approaching a department head with an idea for a class that has never been offered. And it may require considerable skill in getting that person, or a curriculum committee, to see the benefit of presenting such a class to students. Be prepared to deal with a bureaucracy that moves at a snail's pace. The upside is the reward of developing a class to provide students with a topic they may not have considered before.

Community colleges tend to be smaller and can be easier to maneuver from a bureaucratic standpoint. Community colleges also provide shorter two-year degree programs and certificate programs for their students. The need for law-related classes is just as important as at a four-year institution. You may find community college classes to be smaller and more approachable from a teaching standpoint. Because the students will be entering their career field in short order, providing them with an introduction to the legal issues involved may make them more marketable. And that is another positive aspect to present to the administration.

All of these institutions want bragging rights about the employability of their students. And a well-rounded, engaged graduate makes a better employee. In some fields, competition may be intense, and having a student with a more expansive background is important.

The most important part of considering teaching as a pre- or post-retirement option is thinking about what you will bring to the classroom and the students. You do not want to be boring, so it may help to think about which teachers you liked best . . . and why.

Community colleges may also have a paralegal studies program. This is prime real estate for pitching a class. There are specific classes that must be included in the curriculum. This is particularly true if the program is ABA-approved. The ABA has specific requirements for paralegal programs that, while not as stringent as the law school requirements, do require them to provide students with a specific number of study hours in and out of the classroom. This also means more work for the instructors. But, once a course is set up, the ongoing requirements are easier to manage.

All post-secondary education institutions may have an online component for teaching. This presents other opportunities for tech-savvy lawyers. Lee Kolczun, the former chair of the ABA General Practice, Solo, and Small Firm Division, has taught business-related online courses at Lorain County Community College for years. The primary advantage of online courses is that you can teach from anywhere. There is no requirement for you, or the students, to go to the campus. In many scenarios you may never set foot on the campus after the initial discussion.

Having a dependable Internet connection and computer is, of course, essential. And teaching online is different from face-to-face. But if you are comfortable with technology or are willing to learn to be comfortable, online teaching is an option. Further, you may be able to pitch courses to colleges, universities, and community colleges in other cities or states. And you may be able to use the same materials for classes at different institutions. It is something to think about.

# Adult Education Classes

Most cities or counties have some type of adult education classes. However, most of these classes pay instructors little or nothing. Many lawyers use them to market their services. These may provide an opportunity for lawyers who are nearing retirement but anticipate keeping their hand in. Teaching one of these classes, which often last one or two nights, may be a way to market the firm.

# Writing: Content, Freelance, Books, Articles

Finally, another idea is to consider writing. The law firm website is ubiquitous, but, frankly, most of them are not very good. They do more to tout the firm's lawyers and standing in the legal community than marketing to the client base.

Content writing can be thought of as the articles, explanations, and short pieces that some firms include on their websites. Too often those items are not written well, and they do not provide the information needed by a person who is looking for a lawyer.

Law firms with successful websites have realized that quality content is an important part of the firm's overall marketing strategy. This is where you come in. Start by checking out various firm websites. Then contact the managing partner and pitch articles, white papers, or similar writing projects. Explain how your ideas can benefit the firm and enhance its appeal to its client base.

I am not talking about law review articles. This writing is in plain English—clear, concise prose that people want to read and that will impart specific information on specific topics. That means no footnotes, no citations, and no legalese. For example: Why do people need a will?

As a practical matter, most people are afraid of lawyers because they think we will treat them as being stupid. Getting a person over the fear of talking to lawyers will be helpful to any law firm.

Law firms also need to remember that there are now more millennials than Baby Boomers. They are the future client base, and they have specific needs and demands. Writing for different generations is a skill that you can develop. And marketing that skill to law firms is another way to plan your retirement.

Law firms are not the only content market. There is a vast array of magazines, websites, and social media to explore. Consider the magazines, newspapers, websites, social media sites, organizations, alumni associations, and the like with which you are affiliated. Each one is a potential client for your writing. Each one is looking for writers who can pitch a story, deliver on deadline, and work well with the editor.

Every piece of junk mail that comes into your home was written by a writer who was paid for that work. Consider taking classes (online or in person) on copywriting, technical writing, or content writing. Learn to write white papers for businesses and trade magazines.

The American Society of Journalists and Authors (ASJA) holds an annual conference in New York City for freelance writers. These are not novelists or fiction writers. ASJA participants write nonfiction for a plethora of markets. It may be worthwhile to look at other conferences for freelance writers. Or research the subject online and see what piques your fancy.

Some content will require research and interviewing subjects, but that is what we do on a regular basis. You may find assignments in areas with which you are unfamiliar—we all learned to practice law and new areas of law or legal issues throughout our careers. This is not new to us. We understand deadlines and can conform to prescribed publishing standards. Who would have thought that practicing law all these years makes us prime candidates to fill freelance writing assignments?

There is an annual content marketing conference in Cleveland, Ohio. It usually takes place in September, and the conference fees are not cheap. However, put that on the side because the conference attendees, for the most part, are content purchasers, and the conference can be a veritable candy store for content writers. Hobnobbing with the people at the conference while promoting your writing skills makes it possible to make contacts and obtain assignments.

A writer who produces the required content will find a continuous supply of takers. Many people talk about writing, but very few actually write. Considering the various opportunities available for writers may push teaching out of your mind. The whole point is to realize you have options, and they are not limited to the law. Still, that can be difficult to get your head around. Most of us have our identity tied to being a lawyer. And it will take time to see yourself as something other than a lawyer. But it is doable. Another advantage to freelance writing: you can do it from any location, and it does not require a tie!

There is more to retiring from the active practice of law than playing golf or annoying your spouse or significant other. Think of this as the next chapter in your life, one in which you can creatively redesign your future. No one is holding us back except ourselves.

# 17

## RVing for Retiring Lawyers: Driving toward the Future

*by Vicki Levy Eskin*

People take to the road for many reasons. They are known by many names—full-time RVers who have given up bricks and mortar, RV Nomads, Weekenders, Snowbirds, Vacationers, Wanderers, etc. As I move closer and closer to retirement, I suppose I am mostly a wannabe, who takes to the road anywhere from a long weekend to five months out of the year. I've been doing this for nearly a decade and have managed to maintain a vibrant practice, to use the motorhome to combine business and pleasure for hearings or meetings throughout the state and sometimes even out of state, and even to teach continuing legal education courses both in and out of my state. My husband is retired full-time, we have a dog who goes almost everywhere with us, and if we are gone for more than a month, I fly back to my home and office for a week to ten days here and there to attend hearings, meet with clients, and check on home, hearth, and practice. And I love it.

# How Did I Start Out?

After our parents' deaths when they were then around our current ages, my husband and I discussed our thoughts for the future and, in so doing, recognized that our parents' goals had included travel but that they waited until full retirement to start. That plan has merit, but death or disability may often follow one's retirement, so we decided to start earlier than our own parents, who wanted to live their retirement lives much as we are now doing.

As our children were grown and (mostly) out of the nest, we had both become workaholics, with few hobbies and shared interests other than travel and trying local food. So, with retirement looming about eight years ago, we bought a small motorhome and began taking short weekend trips. Almost from the first, I integrated work into our trips. My husband would start out a few hours before me, and I would join him as soon as I could get away from the office. Or I would bring along work to do during our trips.

We are now in our eighth motorhome, a 41-foot model that easily tows a comfortable SUV. We have experimented with different sizes and styles of RVs, motorcycles, towed vehicles, extended stays without interim trips home, monthly week-long trips back to the office, RVing to meet with clients in various locales, and different modes of staying in touch with clients, courts, and staff. By no means do our decisions reflect the best or only way to juggle it all. But, with few exceptions, we have found a way to ease into our retirement in an efficient, cost-effective, enjoyable way and managed to continue to enjoy each other's company, gradually reduce workload, and learn what we like and don't like, and we have no plans to change our travel methods until we physically can no longer continue. And neither of us expects that any time soon, as most modern motorhomes are easy to drive and set up, and some models are even wheelchair accessible if that becomes an issue.

My husband, who managed a family-owned company (not his), officially retired from his full-time work a few years back, experimented with consulting in his field of expertise, and ultimately came to provide me with valuable assistance with some of the work I do. I will address that later. One of the most difficult problems we encountered was my initial inability to separate myself from constant contact with my staff and clients. My husband, who was clearly much wiser than I, rarely took business calls after hours. Not so with me. I struggled with recognizing that I needed to make wiser choices of when, where, and how to continue my work. I have only slightly joked that I took client calls during my parents' funerals, our wedding, major holiday events, and nights and weekends. I felt so very torn between family and work obligations and setting viable boundaries. Though I still struggle with this issue, I have improved my methods so I can juggle it all and continue to enjoy most aspects of my various worlds.

# How Do I Do It?

A lot of people who hear how much time I spend on the road just shake their heads and either say that they envy me but couldn't swing it financially or say that they hope to do it one day but don't sound convinced that day will ever come. I hope this chapter will address some of the important areas that need to be addressed on *how* to ease into retirement and keep one's practice, cash flow, marriage, sense of humor, and sanity (sort of) intact. And not necessarily in that order!

Q. What types of practices can stay vibrant with the principal on the road up to half of the calendar year?

A. My practice is about equally divided between transactional and litigation practice. I am also a certified mediator for civil and appellate matters for the district court of appeals. Although I have a practice in a suburban area, I handle matters throughout the state of Florida. I have yet to encounter a problem with setting hearings around my needs, and with communication with clients becoming so technologically directed, I maintain good relationships with clients, some of whom I've worked with on various matters for more than a decade.

Q. Well, great, but how does one keep a court docket and a client docket without missing dates and aggravating the courts and clients?

A. When I am on the road more than a couple of weeks, I try to schedule minor hearings telephonically. If I absolutely must appear in person, then I do it! It has not been that difficult to schedule around it all. It just takes organization.

I communicate with clients via phone, FaceTime, email, and text and schedule office conferences during trips home about every third or fourth week. During my week at home, I meet with clients virtually back to back, nights and weekends, and in between court hearings. Since I am home alone, no care and feeding of spouse or critter is pulling at me to finish early, though I try to be as efficient as possible with my time and check in with my very tolerant spouse frequently.

Q. What about your family?

A. I am in reverse mode during my home visits. While at home, phone, FaceTime, texts, and emails are with my husband, who has been left to have a peaceful week without me. Lunch and dinner are spent either at my desk or networking or meeting with our children and grandchildren or colleagues and friends. Or I see children and grandchildren while traveling. Occasionally, grandchildren have joined us for short trips. My husband seems pretty happy that I focus more on us when we are away, and he knows that I work hard when I'm at home to get as much as possible done so as not to intrude on our together time. And we schedule my absences at places that he won't mind staying a week, which he fills with activities that he enjoys. I also found a wonderful company that boxes projects with all the necessary materials and tools so he is not at all at a loss to entertain himself in my absence.

Q. Can you do this without a staff? And if you do have staff, what do they handle for you?

A. I think it depends upon your trust level, but at a minimum, having someone monitor the mail is vital. We cover for other lawyers who travel and monitor their mail if they are true solos. I have one full-time assistant, Mane, and one full-time associate, with a few part-time associates and part-time clerks. Both my full-time employees have been involved in the learning process over the past eight years, and we are all generally pretty comfortable deciding what they can handle and what I need to address personally. My assistant has been with me for more than ten years and thus knows what I like and don't like. I trust her and she trusts me. Mane is privy to all incoming and outgoing mail and scans and logs everything in and out. This includes my personal mail, which is forwarded to the office if I am gone for more than three weeks. (Personal mail is held for shorter periods.)

My associate started a year or two after I started traveling. As I move closer and closer to retirement, he drafts most documents for me whether I am in the office or not. For the most part, I still handle communications with my clients as he does with his. He prefers transactional law, though he is quite capable of handling court appearances—and of arguing with opposing counsel or judges that lawyers are not interchangeable, that I am the senior lawyer handling the case and that I am out of state but will be present for a reset. And as most of my cases are with lawyers in the area who are familiar with my travels, the opposing counsel and judges are as reasonable as they can be, and our local judges frown on surprise attack hearings without sufficient notice to counsel. It is rare that my associate has had to handle a hearing on a matter with which he lacked at least a working familiarity, and I am almost always available via phone and Internet before, during, and after hearings where I am not physically present. And importantly, I introduce each and every client to my paralegal and associate and remind them that we are a team and work together on every case to make sure that we provide our clients with peace of mind and access to us when we are needed.

But having a competent, trustworthy staff is critical. Alternatively, there are virtual receptionists and paralegals with whom I have dealt and whom I would trust to handle basic, routine matters.

I also have a few contract lawyers who are quite good and a few local colleagues who would fill in for me if necessary. It is important to have a plan and a backup plan and then a backup plan to the other ones!

I keep more than one calendar to ensure that nothing is overlooked. But if it happens, it isn't for lack of trying.

Q. What sort of technology or equipment do you need while on the road?

A. When I first started traveling via motorhome, I had way more equipment than I use now. I had an all-in-one printer/scanner/copier/fax, a VoIP landline, a PC, an e-reader, a Wi-Fi hotspot, and a cellphone that linked to a laptop. It took up a lot of space but did not always provide for my needs. Gotomypc.com, then as now, gives me the freedom to actually log onto my office PC and into my shared office database to draft or modify documents.

Now, in addition to GoToMyPC, I rely almost solely on an iPad and my cellphone. That's it! I no longer bother with the other cumbersome equipment, though I do have a laptop for backup and for viewing documents too large for me to see well on the iPad. As all my court pleadings are via Internet portal, I do not need written paperwork. And if I do, every RV park where we've stayed has a business office where I can print documents. I bring along a ream of paper, some of my letterhead, printed envelopes in various sizes, padded envelopes, and my FedEx and UPS account numbers. I recently added an all-in-one desktop that doesn't take up a lot of space but admittedly makes documents easier to read and modify due to the size of the monitor and the full-size keyboard. But this is a new addition, and during one of my longest trips, my iPad handled the majority of my needs quite handily. I have chargers at all my perches throughout the motorhome and keep it connected as much as possible so that I don't lose the battery at an inopportune time. The tablet is lightweight and fits easily into my purse and makes handling matters quickly and easily something of a joy! I cannot imagine working on the road without some sort of tablet with its own Internet connection, but I am acquainted with others who aren't as attached to their tablet as I am.

I have reviewed and electronically signed documents with ease, but I have also found the closest printer to print a document requiring an original signature, then turned around and faxed, emailed, or sent back the original with very little inconvenience or expense, as we are rarely far from a place that can provide what is needed to complete the process.

For short trips (under three weeks), our personal mail is held. But when we leave for longer periods, our personal mail is delivered to my office. My paralegal has become quite proficient in determining what need to be scanned and forwarded to me immediately and what can wait until my return.

All bills (business and private) are scanned and emailed to me. And, just as when I am at the office, I set up payment through online banking. The goal is to handle each document once, decide, and move on to the next task.

As most of the courts with which I deal now require online filing with electronic signatures, filing documents from afar is simple. Clients still come by the office to sign notarized documents, or sign and notarize at their convenience, mailing originals to the office. Often, clients do not even realize that I am out of the office for more than two weeks at a time.

Although I occasionally file notices of unavailability where I have a bit of a trust issue with others involved in the case, my staff and I can check my cloud-based calendar (accessible by tablet) at a glance to determine my availability. When we are more than a couple of hours away from my office, there is usually an airport close enough to handle emergency trips, but I have yet to encounter one. I, along with my assistant and associate, receive immediate notice from the court portal of any filed pleading from most courts.

When I travel for three to six months at a time, I purchase economical round-trip tickets from an area where my husband will stay during my absence. Either I shuttle to the airport, or my spouse or assistant transports me. A second vehicle at home is available for my use when I am home.

As I am the only authorized signer on most of my office accounts, I am rather stingy about signing a few extra checks during office time. The checks are retained in an office safe, and a copy of each check is scanned to me before leaving the office. One or two business credit cards stay at the office, and any charges must be approved by me before being tendered.

We recently changed to an invoicing program, which automatically informs me when a client clicks through and pays immediately via credit card, making the ability to monitor cash flow much easier, though online banking and cloud-based billing and time management are also easily accessed.

Q. How do you keep up with CLE and other education requirements?

A. As I mentioned earlier, the motorhome is very handy for attending meetings, hearings, and classes more than an hour or so from my office, but the reality is that I teach enough CLEs, which are more heavily weighted for credits, to keep up. I teach about half of them in person and half via the web. I find that teaching the classes provides multiple benefits: the more I teach, the more carefully I prepare the materials and oral instruction. This helps keep my skills and knowledge current. I receive referrals from those who attend my classes and have cases they feel are above their current skill level. Preparing for various classes helps me to organize pleadings, orders, case law, and treatises together. Not only am I receiving CLE credit without cost, I receive either a modest check or the ability to attend other CLEs without charge. As I am licensed in more than one state and in multiple areas of mediation, paying for courses could be costly, but it is not. And of course, I attend as many ABA free CLEs as possible, particularly when offered through webinars.

Q. Are you able to bill clients or take deductions for travel costs on a regular basis?

A. Of course! The only limitation is my own ability to enter my time and costs. As I do estate planning and probate, my husband and I have developed a side interest in liquidating estates, and the motorhome has made this a cost-effective side venture that helps clients who live out of state and need someone that they trust to handle things locally. And it has been fun for us to learn more about history, collections, and valuation. We've also become less materialistic as we witness the accumulation that some of our projects involve. We've helped prepare for or run estate sales throughout the state. It helps us decide on areas that we would like to visit again or avoid with a passion. As I meet people throughout the country, I am able to refer them to a practitioner who can help them, visit with local lawyers, tour local courthouses, and pick up new clients, Floridians whom I meet along the road.

Q. Well, how do I get started on a shoestring budget?

A. While we have always preferred motorhomes to fifth wheels or campers, our first unit was a used and very inexpensive model. If financed, interest on the motorhome is deductible as a second home! And of course, if used for an extended period, deductions for appropriate use are available, as are the technology expenditures, expendable materials, and postage.

After we paid off the first unit, we upgraded, paid that one off, and so on. We have experimented with both new and used units and have found far better deals and less frustration with previously owned models with low mileage.

Campgrounds are available in price ranges from the cost of a nice latte for one to nice lattes for a small army. There are insurance or clubs that provide discounts. And, when we were in the Southwest, we found that some very nice and free or next-to-free sites were available at small casinos that cater to seniors who RV. Simply signing up for a player's card often provides at least one free buffet, credits to play slot machines without cost, and a free or reduced night, even for those who are not casino devotees. The Golden Age Passport is available for a nominal cost to U.S. citizens upon reaching age 62. With the passport, four people can enter most national parks free or at reduced costs, and camping is available at most parks. Some spots are provided on a first-come, first-served basis, and others must be reserved a year or more in advance. A decision to stay in a state or national park must, however, include a decision on whether full hookup is preferred. I profess to be partial to full hookup, as I like my air conditioning, washer/dryer, shower, and flushable toilet. But this is obviously subject to one's individual preferences.

And there is work camping for those who want to stay in a particular area for several weeks. There are several good sources for this information, and we've met retired lawyers throughout the country who love this option.

Q. Any negatives that I need to consider?

A. No one will ever work as hard or take as much care with your business as you will. So you must be prepared for some reduction in cash flow. And, as with any vacation, the days immediately before departure and after your return will require extra work and extra organization. If you talk too much about your travels, clients and others may worry that you aren't as interested in helping them as they would like or that you are going to retire in full shortly.

I have addressed this by making sure that I return calls promptly, check emails religiously, and assure everyone that I have the best possible life—extremely cooperative staff, court administration, and clients; that I try to bill a minimum of three hours each day; and that I don't plan on ever fully retiring, as this life works for me—it keeps me happy, I still adore my clients, and I've been doing this long enough to know that I really am able to have it all—traveling with my spouse and dog, seeing the country, eating great food, keeping up my legal skills, and, best of all, helping my clients—and I'm never further away than a phone call, text, or email. I can't imagine giving up my RV lifestyle. I just can't wait to get on the road again.

# 18

# Retiring at My Own Speed

## by Wendy Cole Lascher

On July 11, 2018, a couple of days before I turned 68, the Federal Aviation Administration granted me a private pilot's license. In 1973, when I was 23 years old, the State Bar of California had given me a license to practice law.

When I was a new lawyer, I assumed I would never retire. I love the puzzle-solving aspects of my appellate practice. I like lawyers, at least most of them. I liked being mentored when I began my practice, and I like mentoring now. I was and still am active in bar activities. I served as president of a variety of professional associations. I even argued a case in the U.S. Supreme Court. I enjoy the comradeship of many lawyers. My adult identity always was—and still is—being a lawyer. How could I walk away from my identity?

In Justice Frankfurter's (dissenting) words, "Wisdom too often never comes, and so one ought not to reject it merely because it comes late."[1] Sometime during these 45 years of law practice, I finally learned the difference between doing what feels right and doing what I think I "should" do. One item of late-coming wisdom was recognizing that I don't have to say, "I will never retire" or

---

1. Henslee v. Union Planters Nat'l Bank & Trust Co., 335 U.S. 595, 600 (1949).

"I can't wait to retire." I have realized that although cold-turkey retirement is not necessarily a bad thing for those who choose it, there are other options for the rest of us. In fact, it turns out I may have been gradually retiring over the last couple of years without even acknowledging the fact.

# From Small to Big

For most of my career, I practiced in a family-run firm that never had more than four lawyers. We worked out of a beautiful 1894 Victorian building. The other lawyers in my firm were all family or friends, and I still miss our daily outings to play Ms. Pacman or go down the hill to Starbucks.

I was able to bring each of my three sons to the office within a week of their births, and I was known to work with an infant in an open desk drawer when he was not on my lap. Because we lived a short drive from work, once the kids were older and home with a babysitter or in school, I could get away to be with them when I wanted. I could take them to school events, doctor's appointments, and playdates. I could stay home or bring them to work when the sitter had a day off. I could leave early to cook if friends were coming to dinner, take time off for bar activities, get away on short vacations, spend time with extended family, and leave the office for midday walks to the beach.

This is not to say it was always easy to have an easygoing law practice. Like many lawyers, sometimes I had to work in the evening or on the weekend to make up lost time, but at least I was in charge of my schedule. My husband and law partner died in 1991, but I kept the practice going. I turned down at least one serious offer from a major national firm and never really looked at other options. I kept thinking I would never leave the office where we had practiced together because that was what I "should" do.

Eventually, however, the time and stress of dealing with billing clients, keeping up an aging building, maintaining the computer system, handling marketing, and—especially—meeting payroll started to outweigh the fun, let alone the ability to do clients' work effectively. Although I began to realize that I needed to make a change, I waited several years to act. In part I worried that people would think I was a failure if I closed the firm; in part I just did not know what I wanted to do. But one day, when I joked with a friend who was (at the time) in my current firm that the firm should hire me, he told some of the other lawyers there I might be interested, and they made me a partnership offer. So, 37 years after I became a lawyer, at the stage of my career when many of my peers were retiring outright or downsizing to solo practice, I went the other way, joining the largest firm in our tri-county area. Though at 33 lawyers we are not exactly mega, we are definitely the largest fish in the local pond up the coast from Los Angeles.

And I love it. I know every lawyer, secretary, bookkeeper, and support person. I can open the door of my office and step directly outside. Someone else handles hiring and firing, supervising employees, buying supplies, leasing equipment, upgrading computer programs, and so forth. If I disagree with my partners' decisions, which I do occasionally, I also recognize it's the price of the freedom from stress this move gave me. Meanwhile I get to choose my cases, handle them as I think best (with associate support when I need it), mentor younger lawyers, focus on my clients, and make more money than I did when I ran my own firm.

So what does this have to do with retirement?

# Learning to Fly

A couple of years after I moved to the "big" firm, I found the personal relationship I had been hoping for since my husband's death. My boyfriend, a retired journalist, is a private pilot. Early on, he took me to lunch at Catalina Island and on a weekend jaunt to Santa Fe. After a few more flights with him, it occurred to me that I should learn how to land his airplane in case he fell ill, so I signed up for flying lessons. Though parts of ground school befuddled me, and my instructor wondered if I could ever learn even to taxi straight, I kept plodding through the curriculum.

It took me 157 hours in the air with a talented and very patient flight instructor (not my boyfriend, by the way), plus hundreds more hours of classes, seminars, self-study, and absorbing what I observed my boyfriend do as he flew his plane, before I finally passed my written FAA test and checkride. I did not relegate all this learning to evenings and weekends; I just did not come to the office as early in the morning as I used to, or I left a couple of hours early at night, so I could focus on flying.

In other words, instead of retiring, I made a conscious decision to do something for me, rather than my children or my clients or my law partners, in some of the hours I would otherwise have been working. I am not retired; I am just working a little less. I don't see any reason I cannot continue this way for the next few years.

## Stretching My Brain

Early on my instructor explained that for each step of the learning-to-fly process, I had to first learn the procedure, then make that learned procedure a technique in my arsenal, then add finesse. The finesse part goes on forever. I was ready to appreciate this concept because the same thing is true of being a lawyer. I knew the procedures and techniques of practicing law and had acquired a certain degree of finesse, but there comes a time when it's valuable to learn something new.

Until I was in my mid-sixties, I had no exposure to piston engines, no understanding of aerodynamics, no conception of density altitude or how thunderstorms form, no knowledge of airspace or wake turbulence. I did not know how to work a flight calculator or any of the electronic flight bag programs that have supplanted the circular E6B slide rule and changed the process of flight planning. Then all of a sudden I was immersed in all those subjects and more. The only part of learning to fly that was vaguely familiar to me as a lawyer was that I had a sense of how to read the Federal Aviation Regulations. (They are as impenetrable in some places as many other federal regulations.)

The intellectual content is only part of the story. A pilot also has to learn the actual operation of the airplane. I was never naturally coordinated. Learning to open the throttle smoothly, to make a level turn, to adjust pitch and power for landing offered me challenges. The muscle memory is slowly growing.

So for me, learning to fly has been like going back to college—this time to study engineering instead of liberal arts. Engaging my brain in something completely new has proved tremendously refreshing. Since undertaking new mental challenges is supposed to retard the aging process, I expect to stay young(ish) a long time.

## Transferring Skills

After 45 years as a lawyer I know which statutes and cases to cite, what kind of arguments tend to work, and how to talk to clients, judges, and opposing counsel. I do these and other legal tasks more or less automatically, and I hope well, but learning to fly has taught me to rethink the way I practice law. There is so much to pay attention to in the air that you cannot think about deadlines, unreturned phone calls, whining clients, or offensive opponents. Multitasking does not work in the cockpit. Nor does rushing. Another aphorism from my flight instructor: "Slow is smooth, and smooth is fast." That philosophy works in writing briefs, and in life, as well as it does in the airplane.

The same week I wrote this article, I bought a half-interest in a 1965 Cessna 172F. It climbs at 65–80 knots and cruises at 114 knots. That's not fast as private planes go, but my retirement is happening even more slowly.

# 19

## From Courtroom to Cockpit

*by Capt. David R. Hammer*

Every lawyer takes a different route to retirement, and some never retire. A few days ago, I was walking on the dock back to my boat and saw another sailor loading a dock cart. "Looks like you have enough for a couple of weeks of sailing." He smiled ruefully and said, "I wish. Have to get back to the office Monday." I asked what he does, and he replied that he is a lawyer in a small firm in Marin County. I told him that I am a mostly retired lawyer and now live aboard my 42-foot Catalina sailboat and teach sailing, when I am not traveling or at my property on Cozumel, Mexico. He asked how I did it. "I was lucky and got a brain injury case in the 1980s that settled in federal court for a few million." What I told him is true, but that is not how I transitioned from law practice to a boat captain living aboard a yacht on San Francisco Bay and owning property in Mexico.

My life has branched out in several directions, and I have developed a good life as a second act. This year I have enjoyed skiing in Colorado; trips to my property on Cozumel, Mexico; sailing the Bahamas on a 44-foot sailboat, then delivering the boat to Georgia; volunteer work in Las Varas, Mexico, with Rotary International; sailing in a regatta in Malta; chartering a 40-foot catamaran to the Eolian Islands in the Tyrrhenian Sea; and touring Sicily and Sardinia, Italy. And the year is not over. I am now at my property on Cozumel for a week. In August I fly to Hawaii. In September I am renting an RV and touring the Grand Tetons and Yellowstone National Park. In December I return to Cozumel for the holidays. When I am not traveling, I am teaching basic keelboat sailing on San Francisco Bay.

In 1973, the year before I graduated from University of California Hastings College of the Law, I made a tour of all the rural county seats in northern California. I talked with judges and practicing lawyers and chose Weaverville, Trinity County, to open a solo law practice. At the time, I was married, and my wife and I were looking for a small town that was safe to raise children, close to the mountains and lakes, and had the potential for a successful law practice. The first lawyer I met in Weaverville was Al Wilkins. Al graduated from Stanford Law School in 1952 with U.S. Supreme Court Chief Justice William Rehnquist and Justice Sandra Day O'Connor. Al served on the *Stanford Law Review* editorial staff with Rehnquist and O'Connor and, after a few years practicing law in San Diego, moved to Trinity County. Al died in 2016 at age 88. He practiced law almost to the day he died. Although Al never retired from law practice, his life in rural Weaverville allowed him to enjoy the Trinity Alps and the challenges of fighting in court to protect the Trinity River and the Trinity Alps Wilderness. Al introduced me to his junior partner, Jim White, who invited my wife and me to his house overlooking Weaverville. Jim was on *Hastings Law Review* and graduated a few years before me. After Jim and I chatted for a while, he asked, "Would you like to stay for dinner? We're only having hotdogs and beans, but you are welcome to join us." Hotdogs and beans epitomizes the economics of most small-town law practices. The first few years, I got some appointments as a public defender, taught real estate law at night for a community college, joined the Weaverville Rotary Club, attended Naval Reserve weekend training once per month, and worked to develop my practice. After five years, I had two young sons, and

I was not earning as much from my law practice as I expected or wanted. We took a week off and visited my former classmates in more urban areas, including Santa Barbara and Monterey. I learned that although they were making more money, their lifestyle and quality of life was not any better than I had in Weaverville. I returned and extended my office hours, became active in the local bar association, and worked harder. The time and work paid off, and after ten years of practice I was making a decent living. My practice was about 30% real property law, 20% family law, 20% criminal law, 10% personal injury, 10% estate planning and probate, and 10% everything else. Over the years, that changed.

In June 1978, California voters passed Proposition 13. Trinity County immediately quadrupled the Planning Department and County Surveyor's "fees" and enacted some new "fees." I sued the county on behalf of a client who was in the land development business. I contended the new charges were a special tax and required a two-thirds affirmative vote of the electors. The Superior Court granted my client summary judgment, and the county appealed. Thirteen cities and counties joined Trinity County in the appeal. I lost the appeal after the California Supreme Court in two companion cases held that the charges do not constitute a special tax under Proposition 13.[1] But the case gave me recognition. Over the following years, I sued Trinity County a few more times and won. Then in 1998 the Board of Supervisors appointed me as the County Counsel. Some say the board appointed me so I would stop suing the county. Whatever the case, it was a good match, and after the first year they asked me to be full-time as a department head, and my contract was extended after the first four years.

In 1991, I attended the Rotary International Convention in Mexico City. The keynote speaker was the president of Mexico, Carlos Salinas de Gortari. His theme was, "Invest in Mexico." He referred to the negotiations with the United States and Canada to form NAFTA, and he talked about Mexico's trade liberalization,

---

1. Mills v. Trinity Cnty. 108 Cal. App. 3d 657 (1980).

economic deregulation, and privatization of public enterprises. The day after Christmas in 1996, my youngest son and I flew to Cancun, rented a car, and drove to Chetumal, where a real estate broker had a listing on some cheap beachfront property on the peninsula just north of town. The property was worthless with no swimmable beach and an immense heap of trash washed on the shore, two feet high, four feet wide, and as far as we could see along the shore in either direction. We got back in the car and drove to Playa del Carmen, at the time a small resort town south of Cancun, where we took a ferry on New Year's Day to Cozumel. We were impressed with the beaches, growing tourist economy, great scuba diving, and friendly locals. I returned a few months later and started looking at property for sale. My original goal was to build a duplex for a vacation home and extra space for guests or a rental. I got carried away and built a six-unit vacation rental complex, Casa Martillo. Buying and developing property in Mexico was a challenge. Prior to developing Casa Martillo, I had helped clients buy a duplex in San Carlos. My legal education and experience in real estate law were essential in the purchase and development of Casa Martillo. But even with my legal background, I knew I was not qualified to handle the purchase and development of commercial property in Mexico, so I hired a law firm in Mexico City. Over the past 20 years, I have spent a lot of time on Cozumel and have traveled the Yucatan extensively. I manage the reservations myself, and it requires about 15 to 20 hours per week, which is difficult when I am traveling. So now I am listing Casa Martillo for sale. But I will be returning to Cozumel to salsa dance, scuba dive, and enjoy the Mexican food, culture, and margaritas, of course.

In 2004, I retired as County Counsel. With the purchase of my military time credit, I had a total of eleven years credit for retirement with the California Public Employees' Retirement System. During the following four years, I mostly worked as a volunteer on community service projects and international humanitarian projects with Rotary. I kept my license active and performed some pro bono work, a little estate planning, and trust management.

The year following my first retirement, I was the volunteer project manager for the acquisition of property and development of a performing arts center in Weaverville. My comanager was a licensed contractor and close friend. Our nonprofit organization obtained a $1 million grant from the state, which we leveraged into a $1.6 million project. We worked full-time on the project for about a year. My legal knowledge in contracts, real estate, and construction was, in part, why we succeeded in developing the Trinity Alps Performing Arts Center. In addition to being the project manager, I worked with my wife and youngest son on the construction and finishing of the building. Although I did not earn one cent from the project, it was extremely rewarding work.

In 2008, the county asked me to return as an independent contractor to represent Child Protective Services. I had represented CPS during the six years I was County Counsel, but at that time, it was only one of my functions. This was supposed to be part-time and average 30 hours per week. I had an office within the CPS building and was on call 24/7 to process applications for orders to detain a child. About once a month I would receive a call in the middle of the night from a social worker, help draft a declaration, then call a judge at home to get an order within four hours of detaining the child. The five years I represented CPS were some of the most rewarding years of my law career. I viewed every case as a win. In most cases, the law requires that the parent or parents be offered services to help overcome the problems that led to the removal of the child. If the parents are successful, the child is returned to a better home. If the parents fail reunification, parental rights are usually terminated, and the first option is adoption. In those cases, the child is given a new family and a second chance to have a stable home. Either way, the child wins. One important aspect of representing CPS after more than 30 years of law practice is the ability to research and know the law and convey that knowledge to the judge and social workers. One case I will never forget. The trial judge erroneously granted the mother reunification services after her parental rights had been terminated for a sibling. I filed an appeal and won. The attitude of the judge in future cases was more circumspect.

In February 2013, I celebrated my 68th birthday. There were several places to go and things to do on my bucket list, so I retired for the second time. That year I immunized children against polio and worked on a school project in Togo, West Africa, with Rotary International; competed in an international table tennis tournament in Croatia; chartered a catamaran in the Croatian islands; visited Mexico several times; backpacked in the Trinity Alps; skied Mount Shasta; scuba dived; taught salsa dancing; and took vocal lessons.

For many years I had yearned to sail the seas on my own boat. I have been sailing since I was about 12 and had owned and raced many boats from 10 to 25 feet in length. I also have bareboat chartered 45-foot catamarans and sailed many other boats. After earning my BA from Long Beach State in 1966, I got my commission as an ensign in the Navy and spent the next 18 months aboard a 42,000-ton fleet oiler and became a qualified bridge officer. So it is no surprise that in 2015 I purchased a 42-foot Catalina sailboat in San Diego, sailed it to San Francisco, and moved aboard. At the same time, I started studying for a merchant marine captain's license. The written examination for the license is six modules with 200 questions and takes about four hours. I was required to document 720 days of sea time, including 180 days of sailing. Candidates are also required to complete first aid/CPR, a security clearance, and a drug test. I took an online course and spent several months getting my sea time records from the Navy. It took almost two years to obtain my 100-ton sail and power U.S. Coast Guard Merchant Marine Master license. I am now qualified to command a boat about the size of a San Francisco ferry, under sail or power, within 200 miles of the shore. I am also a certified American Sailing Association instructor for basic keelboats and teach for Tradewinds Sailing School, in Richmond, California. The certification required another two-day course and written examination and a demonstrated ability to sail and teach sailing. So now I get paid for participating in my favorite sport. My legal expertise did not help me know the maritime rules and laws, but the analytical approach is the same as in the other areas of law, and I had an advantage over the other candidates taking the exams.

I have kept my bar license active and last year closed a $4.6 million intestate probate in Alameda County that added to my retirement fund.

From my perspective, the volunteer work I have done through Rotary and my travels have helped me in my law career. This is particularly true regarding my work in family law and representing CPS. I became more compassionate from helping children around the world. The community service and volunteer work through Rotary Club gave me credibility in my small town and a reputation of integrity. These are, of course, essential to a successful law practice.

Some friends have told me I should have run for Superior Court Judge. I thought about running for many years, but the timing was never right. Before the consolidation of the courts, I knew I did not want to be a municipal court judge because trying DUI, fishing tickets, and small claims cases four days a week did not appeal to me. Sometimes, I regret not running for judge, but I have had a very rewarding law career. If had it to do all over again, I don't think I would have changed what I did. If I were advising a solo practitioner in his or her fifties, I would say: "Look at ways to serve your community, make a name for yourself, and provide public service." That, in part, is why I was appointed County Counsel. In 1974, I chose to become a big frog in a small pond. I don't regret that decision.

One thing I think is very important about the transition into retirement is to keep physically fit. I exercise daily, eat a hamburger and fries once a year on July 4, do not smoke, and limit my beer intake. Staying healthy and active is a necessity for a happy retirement.

# 20

## Picture This: The Journey to My Second Act

*by Victoria L. Herring*

Paul Simon's "Kodachrome" was the hit song the summer I started law school, but I didn't know that it would foretell my future. Graduating from law school in 1976, I was looking forward to an entire professional life full of practicing law. My father was a lawyer, and I'd wanted to be one, just like him, since I was five. Even though I would flirt with being a teacher, archaeologist, architect, and looping back to being a teacher, I ultimately would settle on a career in law. Each career option involved some element of creativity and a responsibility for protecting and advancing knowledge and the interests of others. Even as I thought of these careers, during my youth and into young adulthood I continued to be involved in the visual arts, either through oil or acrylic painting or in my own rudimentary photography (it helped that my father also enjoyed photography and was quite good). I attended a liberal arts college that provided me with an excellent education and life skills that enabled me to stay involved in the arts, including photography.

After some time in the real post-college world, I attended Drake University Law School as a nontraditional student. I was drawn to Drake because of its practical approach to training lawyers. This meant that students not only would be engaged in lecture and book learning of legal principles and methods but also would be able to dip our toes into the practice. While a law student, I was able to clerk for a judge who treated the opportunity as a teaching moment. I would watch a case unfold in his courtroom, and then he and I would sit and discuss how each side handled the case and what might be the best outcome. The decision was always his, but the discussions taught me a lot about what a judge would consider in rendering a decision. I also worked in the legal clinic the law school sponsored, in the satellite housed in the student union at Iowa State University. There I dealt with unmarried fathers' rights issues, small claims, contract, and other types of basic disputes that at times allowed me to actually represent someone in court. Those opportunities whetted my appetite for more litigation experience.

Clerking during law school in a small law office led to being hired as an associate in a medium-sized law firm handling civil matters. The firm had a fairly old-fashioned view of how associates should progress, and I was older and eager and wanted to be more involved with clients and actual litigation, rather than reading abstracts and researching odd questions about estates and trusts. After a few years in that practice, I left and applied for a job with the Iowa Attorney General's office. Fortunately, I was hired to work as an assistant attorney general assigned to the civil rights division. That assignment fit my desire to do good and be more involved in litigation.

As its lawyer, I was housed with the Iowa Civil Rights Commission (ICRC) for about four years, and it was there that I found my calling. I was able to work in an area of great interest to me, protecting and advancing the various civil rights of the people of Iowa, handling race discrimination cases, sex discrimination cases, and sexual harassment and other such cases, and, as the law developed, disability and other types of cases.

As an assistant attorney general with the ICRC, I became a full-fledged litigator, working on every step of a case from interviewing witnesses and researching the law to presenting the case in a hearing before a hearing officer and the commission and in district court and arguing the merits of the commission's decisions on appeal. It was a great job and very fulfilling, and I was able to work and travel throughout the state, visiting places that I might never have gone to otherwise. My camera would accompany me on these travels, and I would photograph what I saw and experienced, mainly as a pastime. Before long, I had enough experience as a litigator and expertise in the area of civil rights and discrimination that I could move out of government into the private practice of law. Or so I hoped.

In late 1983, not finding an associate position in an established firm, I opened my own office as a solo. Of course, when I sent out my announcements and found an office I could afford to rent, I was fortunate to have many friends who sustained me with tasks in bread-and-butter areas of the law—family law, contracts, small claims, real estate, probate, etc. Because of my expertise with civil rights and discrimination law, I was hired to assist a local city civil rights commission and assist with other cases in that area that came to me. For almost 20 years, practice as a solo was fantastic, even as I shared my energies with three stepchildren, two children, cats, and a husband. I enjoyed the area of law I was practicing in, the demanding and interesting nature of the cases, helping people to protect their rights, and all the things that make practicing law fulfilling. And through these years I continued to hone my talents as a photographer, taking classes, improving my equipment, taking pictures on various family trips, using my talent in photography to fulfill my right-brain needs, but still thinking of it as a pastime and not a career option.

And then the day came in the mid-2000s when I decided that I really did not want to practice as I had been—at one point I was employing three paralegals and three law clerks and handling a number of cases in jury trials and litigation, some held over multiple weeks. The challenges of the cases and running the law firm were great and fulfilling for a time. But it became overwhelming to handle all this as a solo, and I decided to pull back from more involved cases, winnowing my excellent staff through attrition, and focusing on something I had enjoyed for many years—the art of photography.

I continued to practice law as a solo with a pared-down staff and caseload. I shifted to an hourly pay model of client representation: a business decision because I did not have the financial resources to underwrite substantive litigation and wanted a way to limit cases to only those where clients had skin in the game. As a result, I ended up with relatively few new cases, but that allowed me to become more involved with photography.

Ever since I was a child, I enjoyed photography and took pictures despite the fact that in those days one sent the film away to be developed, a fairly expensive process. In college, I took a class in photography and learned a bit about developing my own photographs but still mainly sent them away for developing and printing. The rolls and rolls of film taken during those business trips and family vacations made me wish I'd invested in Kodak stock.

Pulling back from practicing law increased my involvement in photography. In 2005, I shot one of the Henry Moore sculptures in front of the Meier Wing of the Des Moines Art Center. It was a perfect day, the Moore piece's bronze casting turning red in the light, the Meier wing blazing white, and the sky clear and bright. I entered it into a competition in Des Moines, was one of the finalists, and had my image displayed. As a normal human being, I was gratified and excited about this notice, which contrasted with the long, tedious, and frequently unfulfilling nature of results in the legal practice. Even winning cases didn't excite me as much as my photograph being hailed as an exemplar of Des Moines.

That was the spark. I'm normal, so praise and accolades frequently encourage and prompt me to do more. Not that I wasn't finding similar positive feedback from the practice of law at times, but this was something new and different, and it spoke to an emotional part of me that wasn't nurtured quite enough by the law. I loved the intellectual challenge of the law and the sense of doing good for others, but I lacked a sense of emotional fulfillment. So I decided to become more involved in my avocation. I purchased a better camera, took more photographs, attended classes, and subscribed to too many magazines to try to learn about techniques and how best to become an accomplished photographer. I had and have no interest in the art of portrait photography but find challenge and excitement in photographs of life in the real world—people, places, buildings, and things that offer an interesting pattern or a different view.

Fortunately for me, digital photography became more widespread and improved in quality over the years, so that by the time I really started to focus my attention on photography as a profession, using a digital camera to take photos and a computer to process them was a legitimate choice to make. Using digital methods certainly also made it quite easy to be a photographer and take pictures and work with them. Twenty years as an Apple aficionado would make using my Apple computers, with their focus on graphics and design, to work with digital images a no-brainer. So I continued to travel and take pictures, to stay home and take pictures, and to work with the hundreds and then thousands of photographs I was taking with my digital camera. I was still practicing law but handling fewer and fewer cases because I had left a contingency fee practice and billed hourly. That's a fairly natural way to limit one's practice.

I decided that I'd keep practicing law, but my hobby would be my avocation and I'd try to become better at it. I fully expected to continue this way and retire from being a lawyer in the far distant future. So I upgraded my camera equipment again, upgraded my computer and software (using Apple computers, I bought Aperture and tried to learn how to organize and edit images for the maximum effect), and kept traveling with my husband and our kids. We would use the slow holiday period at year's end to take everyone somewhere overseas or in the western United States. Then I took a fateful trip, alone, to Asia.

Back in 2001, some friends had wanted to hike in the country of Bhutan, and we went through with all the difficult arrangements, took our shots, and worked to build up our stamina. I planned not only to hike but also to practice my photography along the way. We were all excited to go, only to have our excitement stunted by the events of 9/11. We each returned to our jobs and careers, disappointed but realizing that it just wasn't a good time to travel thousands of miles away to an unknown country. Time went on, and a few years later I again became interested in Bhutan, but this time with the thought of taking a photography workshop, seeing the people and country, and learning better ways to take photographs. In fact, 2006 was to be my photographic coming-out party. That year was filled with photography-centered events. I continued to practice law but had better control over fewer cases.

Loving Venice, I traveled there in January 2006, took a two-day photography workshop, and expanded my knowledge and horizons. Then in May I went to Bhutan for a very special and literally eye-opening photographic workshop over a two-week period of driving with 13 other people through the country on its passable road (yes, it has one road, which bisects the country from east to west), with stop-offs for Bangkok prior to and Beijing at the end of the trip. In the fall it was back to Venice for a week with women friends exploring the city, again taking a day out for another workshop with my teacher of earlier that year. There is something about being involved in a fairly structured setting, such as tutelage or a workshop, that brings out the best in you as a photographer and expands your reach. At least that's true in my case.

When I returned from Italy and Bhutan, I wondered if I couldn't make this avocation financially sustain itself, at least in part. I could keep my day job but become increasingly involved in fine art photography as a business. I was also motivated by the positive feedback and the enjoyment others got from my images.

With the help of friends, I became involved in a gallery in the East Village of Des Moines; I displayed some of my images there and in another gallery in another city over several years. I also entered photography competitions and was juried into recognized art shows in the Des Moines area. I started to build not only my inventory of images but also the variety of materials and display mechanisms needed to have an attractive and professional-looking photographic presentation at these shows.

It certainly helped to have friends at this time. Just as my friends sustained and supported me when I entered the solo practice of law many years ago, they did likewise with my launch into the field of photographic art. Not that my images weren't or aren't worth purchasing, but as with anything else, the support and encouragement of friends meant a great deal. One allowed me to set up a tent in front of her shop during the downtown farmer's market; although it is not the perfect venue for art sales, I was and am proud of what I accomplished that summer. Other friends bought images, both matted and framed, as well as cards; they placed orders and generally kept me positive about this shift in my focus.

By this time, I had been juried into shows in other Midwestern cities and was practicing law as well, but on a more limited scale. When I began to operate my law practice from home, I completed what cases I could and encouraged and assisted some clients to find and retain new counsel; our children being in their teens, I thought it was best to be available at home and not rushing off to a law office elsewhere. The steady growth of my photography business (not profit, but growth nonetheless) added to my contentment.

Over the next few years I continued along this path. Our family enjoyed travel, and I kept shooting photographs, returning home with one or two thousand images to review and choose from, to work with on the computer, and then to print. When not traveling and otherwise involved in photography, I practiced law and worked on civil rights and discrimination cases in the agencies, in federal court, and on appeal. My left brain was engaged, my right brain was happy.

Finding more success from contests and various art shows in Iowa and around the Midwest was certainly more enjoyable than dealing with contentious people in litigation. I created a business, JourneyZing (journeyzing.com), to display and market my images. And as my husband and I traveled through parts of the world beyond Iowa—Wales, Italy, France, Portugal, Turkey, Spain, and here and there in South America—I tried to take as many photographs as possible to record the places and people we saw. Doing so meant that then I had to sift through thousands of images to find the true best ten to twenty to share with others.

About five years ago, I started exploring how to have my various photographs displayed outside of my home. It makes no sense to take pictures and create art and then consign them to the basement. So I met with some friends and other resources over a few years, and ultimately four of us decided to open an art gallery where they could display and sell their paintings, jewelry, and fiber arts, and I could display and sell my photographs, all of us acting as partners in the endeavor. This gallery, Artisan Gallery 218 (artisangallery218.com), is located in a quaint shopping district called Valley Junction near Des Moines and benefits from the natural tourism that flourishes there. Over the past three years, the gallery has grown to have a full group of skilled artisans of all types. We complement each other and work together not only to be successful in the business of art but also to educate others about the importance of art in their lives.

I am now at the point where I have made the firm decision to retire as an attorney, focusing my attention on improving my photographic skills and marketing and selling my work. Fortunately, the state of Iowa has recognized that many lawyers, particularly of the Boomer generation, need or want to retire, and the supreme court has passed new rules that permit a lawyer to formally retire.[1]

---

1. *Succession Planning by Iowa Attorneys*, IOWA JUDICIAL BRANCH, https://www.iowa courts.gov/opr/attorneys/attorney-practice/practice-information/retirement (last accessed Feb. 7, 2019).

The skills one learns to become a lawyer and as one practices as a lawyer are excellent for many purposes, not just the practice of law. They include civility in dealings with others, honesty in those dealings and in your life and practice, dedication to your clients, a sense of honor, and knowledge of the value of hard work on behalf of your clients. All of those skills are certainly useful in the world of creating art and the business of selling it. And, actually, in life in general. So I haven't really left the law totally, just refocused my energies and given up my ability to practice as a lawyer. But the skills remain with me, and I hope to be able to turn them to a good purpose. It's time to read the writing on the wall.

## PRACTICAL STEPS TO A SECOND ACT

When you're looking to move to the latter part of your life, where you leave the law practice behind and try to focus your energies on what you would love to do with your life, there are some practical steps you need to take.

If you are leaving a firm or established entity, research what benefits you can retain in your second act (e.g., health benefits), because, unless you are of Medicare age or taking Social Security, you'll need to figure out how to finance those needs. Given what normally happens in the latter part of your life, you'll find increasing demands on your physical, mental, and dental health, and you'll need to find methods of dealing with them that won't stress your finances. You will no longer have the cushion of an earned income or benefits to look to, and planning for those expenses is crucial.

You should only take the leap if this is something that would fulfill you much more than the legal practice and camaraderie you get from that. You need to be doing something you would truly love to do, something that will challenge you and keep you interested and interesting for the remainder of your life. If you don't really love the practice of law as you now do it, maybe a shift in emphasis, area of practice, or whom you work with would suffice? There's no need to leave the practice of law for a second act doing something totally different if you can find a different focus to reinvigorate your involvement with the law: pro bono work, legal aid, or a nonprofit might be the way to practice law and remain fulfilled.

If you do find something nonlegal that captures your excitement and imagination, then perhaps do a trial run to make sure it's something you want to become the focus of your life. I learned that I love to take and work with photographs and to travel but that the involvement in a gallery, where I would have to undertake retail sales, was not my cup of tea. That is probably mainly because I've practiced law and been in total charge of my life for almost forty years and am not used to having a set work schedule. The people and ambiance of the gallery are fine; it was my feeling of being tied to a place that causes the problem. So test out what it is you want to do and see if it's right for you. As is often said, "don't quit your day job."

See if you can take a sabbatical from the law practice and return to it if your new life just isn't right for you. That may take working out an arrangement with your firm and figuring out how you will maintain your active license to practice and health care benefits, but that sort of trial run might be a good idea.

# Part VI

# Strategizing Your Social Security Claim

Solo and small firm lawyers' financial resources are all over the land-scape, some having had the good fortune to invest and save, others living day-to-day, and everyone else somewhere in between. The only constant is that all of them will have some amount of Social Security benefits, assuming they've paid in enough and live long enough.

**Chapter 21**
Social Security Benefits for You and Your Family
*Avram L. Sacks*

# 21

# Social Security Benefits for You and Your Family

*by Avram L. Sacks*

## Introduction

If you are thinking about retirement, you should also be considering how income from Social Security Retirement Insurance Benefits (RIB) will be a part of your income flow after retirement. So, why is Social Security important? Although these benefits will not provide a major source of post-retirement income for practitioners who have been used to six-figure incomes for most of their careers, Social Security retirement benefits still account, on average, for 15% of the post-retirement income for retirees in the top economic quintile (for individuals age 65 and over with average annual lifetime income in excess of $72,129 according to the Social Security Administration (SSA, Office of Policy, *Income of the Aged Chartbook*, 2014, p. 17, https://www.ssa.gov/policy/docs/chartbooks/income_aged/2014/iac14.pdf)). Stated differently, for individuals reaching age 62 in 2018 with career average indexed earnings of $82,000, Social Security retirement benefits replace just over one-third (36%) of an individual's pre-retirement earnings. Individuals reaching age 62 in 2018 with career average indexed earnings of $125,500 can expect that 29% of their pre-retirement earnings will be replaced with a Social Security retirement benefit.

However, how one strategizes the timing of his or her claim for a Social Security retirement benefit could make a difference of as much as $100,000 to $200,000 in terms of the present value of the amount of cumulative household benefit that one can expect to receive together with a spouse over their anticipated lifetimes. Although maximizing one's retirement benefits may take a back seat to other considerations, such as a desire to travel, preserve other retirement funds, etc., knowing how the timing of one's claim for retirement benefit can impact the expected amount of benefits will enable one to make a more fully informed decision about when to claim Social Security retirement benefits.

In order to help *you* make a more fully informed decision about *your* claim for a Social Security retirement benefit, this chapter will examine

- how one becomes entitled to a Social Security retirement benefit,
- the difference between "early" and "full" retirement,
- how a retirement benefit is calculated,
- the types of benefits available to a retiree's dependents and survivors,
- factors that can decrease or increase benefits,
- the impact on a benefit if one continues to work after becoming entitled to a benefit,
- taxation of benefits,
- the impact of various benefit claiming strategies, and
- how to maximize retirement benefit and where to go for more information.

Whole books have been written on this subject; thus, it will not be possible to cover each of these topics in great depth. However, it is hoped that you will at least become sufficiently aware of the major issues, in order that you will be able make an intelligent decision about your own application for a Social Security retirement benefit.

# Benefit Eligibility

In order to receive a Social Security retirement benefit on one's own earnings record, one must be insured under the Social Security Act and must also have attained age 62. (As will be discussed below, other types of insured Social Security benefits are available prior to this age.) To be insured, one must be credited with 40 quarters of coverage (QCs). One earns a QC by having earnings subject to Social Security tax of at least a minimum amount within a calendar year. That amount increases annually. For example, the amount of earnings required for a QC in 2018 is $1,320. This amount increases to $1,360 for 2019. Thus, if one has earnings of at least $5,280 for 2018, he or she will have earned four QCs. A maximum of four QCs may be earned in any one calendar year, and the amount needed to earn one QC need not be earned in each calendar quarter. It can all be earned in one day, but a quarter may not be credited until the end of the calendar period tied to that quarter. For example, although one might have earned $6,000 in January 2019, which is sufficient for crediting all four quarters, the first quarter is not credited until the end of March, the second is not credited until the end of June, and so on. A chart showing the amount of earnings required to earn a QC in prior years appears at https://secure.ssa.gov/poms.nsf/lnx/0300301250. For years prior to 1978, refer to https://secure.ssa.gov/poms.nsf/lnx/0300301301.

It is not enough to have earnings above a certain threshold in order to earn a QC. One must have earnings that were subject to tax under FICA (Federal Insurance Contributions Act) or SECA (Self-Employed Contributions Act). Individuals who worked primarily in the public sector or abroad may not have the requisite number of QCs. However, in lieu of Social Security benefits, these individuals may be entitled to a pension that pays better than a Social Security benefit.

Although eligibility is assured with 40 QCs, an application for retirement benefits (referred to as "old-age" benefits by the Social

Security Act) must be submitted in order to become "entitled" to the benefit. The application may be submitted online, by telephone, or at your local field office. The location of the local field office for your area may be determined using the SSA's online locator (https://www.ssa.gov/locator). Although an appointment is not necessary, it is recommended in order to avoid a wait that could last hours at your local field office. If you want to apply online, you should indicate in the "remarks" section near the end of the form the month for which the first payment should be made. Because payments are made one month in arrears, if you want payment to begin, let's say, *for* June 2019, you should indicate that the first payment should be for June 2019, to be received in July 2019.

You may apply for a benefit up to four months in advance of the month for which payment is to be made. However, retirement benefits may only be paid retroactively for up to six months, and cannot be paid retroactively for any month for which benefits are reduced due to "early claiming," which will be discussed in the next section.

# The Difference between Early and Full Retirement

An insured worker may claim a Social Security retirement benefit as early as age 62, although, one must be at age 62 throughout a month in order to receive a benefit exactly at age 62. A widow(er) insured on the account of his or her deceased spouse may claim a widow(er)'s benefit as early as age 60 and if the widow(er) is disabled and unable to work, he or she may claim a disabled widow(er)'s benefit as early as age 50. Note, however, that retirement benefits will be "actuarially" reduced if claimed prior to full retirement age (FRA), and a worker receiving any benefit prior to FRA will experience a reduction in that benefit if the worker continues to work and has earnings over a stated threshold. Any claim for benefits prior to FRA is considered to be "early retirement." Spousal benefits claimed prior to FRA are not reduced for early retirement if the spouse has in his or her care a minor child under age 16 or an older child who has been determined to be disabled under the Social Security Act. For surviving spouses with a minor child under age 16 or a disabled child who is older, a special benefit is available that is not subject to actuarial reduction. See the discussion, below, regarding mother's and father's benefits.

For many years, FRA was 65. However, under the Social Security Amendments of 1983, Congress increased that age to 67, phasing in the increase over a 22-year period, beginning in 2003 for those born after January 1, 1938. Those approaching FRA in 2019 can expect to attain FRA at 66. Retirement age will begin to increase to 67 at the rate of two months per year, beginning with those born after January 1, 1955.

The following chart shows what age is FRA for an individual given that individual's date of birth.

| If birth date is . . . | Then FRA is . . . |
|---|---|
| 1/2/38–1/1/39 (age 62 in 2000) | 65 years and 2 months |
| 1/2/39–1/1/40 (age 62 in 2001) | 65 years and 4 months |
| 1/2/40–1/1/41 (age 62 in 2002) | 65 years and 6 months |
| 1/2/41–1/1/42 (age 62 in 2003) | 65 years and 8 months |
| 1/2/42–1/1/43 (age 62 in 2004) | 65 years and 10 months |
| 1/2/43–1/1/55 (age 62 in 2005–2016) | 66 years |
| 1/2/55–1/1/56 (age 62 in 2017) | 66 years and 2 months |
| 1/2/56–1/1/57 (age 62 in 2018) | 66 years and 4 months |
| 1/2/57–1/1/58 (age 62 in 2019) | 66 years and 6 months |
| 1/2/58–1/1/59 (age 62 in 2020) | 66 years and 8 months |
| 1/2/59–1/1/60 (age 62 in 2021) | 66 years and 10 months |
| 1/2/60 and later (age 62 in 2022 and beyond) | 67 years |

Although benefits are decreased for any worker who first claims a benefit prior to FRA, benefits are also *increased* if an individual delays his or her claim past FRA.

The decrease is $5/9 \times 1\%$ for each month a benefit is claimed early, up to the first 36 months, and is an additional $5/12$ of 1% for each month thereafter. Thus, for an individual with a FRA of 66 and claiming exactly at age 62, the reduction will be 25%, to reflect a 48-month reduction period. Note that for most people claiming at age 62, the reduction will be slightly less than that: 24.58%, to reflect a 47-month reduction period. This reflects two rules that govern the payment of Social Security retirement benefits: (1) an individual attains a given age on the day *before* the anniversary of their birth, and (2) one must be at age 62 throughout an entire month in order to receive a benefit for that month. Thus, only individuals born on the *second* day of the month will be able to claim a benefit in the month they reach age 62. All others, including those born on the first day of the month, will not be able to begin to receive a benefit until the month *after* the month in which age 62 is attained. (An individual born on the first day of the month actually attains age 62 in the prior month!)

If a worker chooses to delay a claim for retirement benefits beyond the month in which FRA is attained, the benefit will be increased by $2/3$ of 1% for each month of delay up to age 70. These increases are referred to as "delayed retirement credits" (DRCs). Because there is no increase in the benefit if its claim is delayed beyond age 70, there is no advantage in delaying a claim for retirement benefits past age 70.

# How a Benefit Is Calculated

In order to better understand how one's earnings impact the benefit one receives, it helps to pull back the curtain and understand how a benefit is calculated.

A Social Security benefit is based on a complex statutory formula that is progressive and replaces a higher proportion of pre-retirement earnings for workers with lower lifetime earnings than for workers with higher lifetime earnings. Although, regardless of where one is situated in the spectrum of lifetime earnings, the more one has earned, the more one will receive as a benefit.

As discussed below, "earnings" refers to earnings that were subject to Social Security tax, i.e., tax under FICA or SECA during a worker's career. Such earnings are also called "covered earnings." Investment earnings as well as earnings from employment not subject to Social Security tax, such as state or local government employment and foreign employment, are not covered earnings and will not be utilized in the calculation of the benefit. Additionally, earnings above the level of earnings subject to Social Security tax, the wage base, are not counted in the calculation of the benefit. (The wage base was $128,400 in 2018 and is $132,900 for 2019.) Self-employed individuals counting on a relatively large Social Security benefit due to a lifetime of high earnings may be surprised to discover that their Social Security benefit is relatively low if their accountant has structured their earnings so as to result in a low tax liability under SECA. In the discussion below, unless otherwise indicated, when we refer to earnings, we are referring only to covered earnings.

A Social Security retirement benefit amount is based on the highest 35 years of a worker's indexed earnings and is calculated in a three-step process. In step 1, a worker's annual earnings are indexed to national average wages for the year in which the worker reaches age 60. In step 2, the worker's highest 35 years of indexed earnings are summed and divided by the number of months in that period (420) to yield a number called "average indexed monthly earnings" or AIME. In step 3, the AIME is converted to a number termed the "Primary Insurance Amount" (PIA). The conversion is accomplished by multiplying successively higher portions of AIME by successively smaller percentages to yield the PIA. The percentages, which are fixed by statute, are 90%, 32% and 15%. The portions to be multiplied are determined by "bend points," which increase annually with increases in national average wages. The bend points used for any given worker are the bend points for the year in which a worker reaches age 62. The calculation can best be illustrated by an example.

Let's assume you will retire at age 66 in 2019, and let's further assume that your average indexed monthly earnings are $6,000. If you reach age 66 in 2019, you would have reached age 62 in 2015. The applicable bend points are the bend points for 2015, which are $826 and $4,980. Thus, the first $826 of the AIME is multiplied by 90%, the next portion of AIME ($4,980 − $826 = $4,154) is multiplied by 32%, and the remaining portion of AIME ($6,000 − $4,980 = $1,020) is multiplied by 15%. The three products are summed to yield the PIA:

$$0.90 \times \$826 = \$743.40$$

$$0.32 \times (\$4,980 - \$826) = 0.32 \times \$4,154 = \$1,329.28$$

$$0.15 \times (\$6,000 - \$4,980) = 0.15 \times \$1,020 = \$153$$

$$\text{PIA} = \$743.40 + \$1,329.28 + \$153.00 = \$2,225.68,$$
which is then rounded down to the nearest $0.10, as required by law, to yield $2,225.60.

PIAs are also subject to annual increases due to application of the cost-of-living adjustment (COLA) from age 62. Thus, the actual benefit at age 66 will reflect annual COLAs since 2015 of 0%, 0.3%, 2.0% and 2.8%. Upon application of the COLAs, the PIA increases to $2,340.50 for 2019. The actual benefit that is payable rounds down the PIA to the nearest whole dollar to yield a monthly benefit of $2,340 for a worker reaching age 66 in 2019 with an AIME of $6,000.

If a worker continues to work past FRA, annual earnings in subsequent years, without indexing, will be used for the AIME calculation, so long as the earnings are higher than the lowest annual indexed earnings in the 35 years of indexed earnings that were initially used to calculate the AIME. In that circumstance, the lowest of the 35 years of annual earnings previously used for the calculation is removed, and the higher, more recent annual earnings are added to the calculation. Thus, if you continue to work after reaching age 62, your PIA will be recomputed each year you have earnings in excess of the lowest of the indexed annual earnings used for the computation in the prior year. However, the bend points for the year in which age 62 is attained will be used for all computations, and the final result will be increased by any COLAs that are applicable for years after age 62 is attained. Because 35 years of earnings are always used for the calculation, each additional year of earnings, even if at a very high earnings level, will only have a modest impact on the increase in the AIME and an even more modest impact on the PIA (because increases at levels above the second bend point will be added to the benefit amount at the rate of only 15%).

It is important to remember that a PIA is not necessarily the benefit amount. It *can* be the benefit amount if the benefit is first claimed at FRA and if there are no other factors present that might serve to reduce the benefit. But, in many cases, determining the PIA is only the starting point for determining the actual benefit amount. As will be seen below, many factors can serve to reduce or increase the actual benefit that is paid. However, before looking at those factors, it will be helpful to first understand the benefits that may be available to the dependents and survivors of an insured wage earner.

# Benefits Available to Dependents and Survivors

Social Security benefits are available not only for insured workers but also potentially to their dependents. Spouses, ex-spouses, minor or disabled adult children, and dependent parents of an insured worker may all be eligible to receive a Social Security benefit on the earnings record of an insured worker if that worker files for and becomes eligible to receive a Social Security retirement or disability benefit or dies. When a benefit is paid to a family member on the earnings record of an insured worker, the benefit is known as an "auxiliary" benefit. The circumstances under which these individuals may qualify for an auxiliary benefit are described below.

In all cases, except with respect to widow(er)'s benefit, the amount of the benefit is a percentage of the PIA of the insured worker, regardless of when the insured worker claimed his or her benefit. These percentages range from 50% to 100% of the insured worker's PIA but are also subject to reduction in the case of a spousal or widow(er)'s benefit if claimed before the dependent reaches his or her own FRA. As will be discussed in other sections below, these benefits may also be reduced if received by a dependent below FRA who is working and has earnings above certain thresholds or is receiving a pension based on noncovered earnings.

The different types of auxiliary benefits, who may qualify to receive them, and the amount of the benefit are discussed in each subsection below.

## Spouses

A spousal benefit is available to the spouse of an insured worker, beginning at age 62 (or earlier if the spouse has in his or her care a child of the insured under age 16 or disabled). However, in order to be eligible for the benefit, the insured worker must already be "entitled" to retirement or disability benefits. As previously discussed, to be "entitled" to a benefit means that the person is eligible to receive the benefit and has submitted an application for the benefit.

So, who is a "spouse"? To be a spouse, the applicant for a spousal benefit must be regarded as married under the laws of the state in which the insured had a permanent home at the time of the claim for spousal benefits and must meet one of the following criteria:

(1) the marriage has lasted for at least one year (the requirement is met throughout the month in which the first anniversary of the marriage occurs), (2) the spouse is the natural parent of the insured's child, or (3) the applicant, in the month prior to the month of marriage, would have been entitled to a wife's, husband's, widow's, widower's, parent's, or disabled child's benefit, or annuity payments under the Railroad Retirement Act for widows, widowers, parents, or children 18 years of age or older.

Note that even if the marriage is not valid under state law, it may still be deemed to be valid if, in good faith, the parties went through a marriage ceremony that would have resulted in a valid marriage but for a legal impediment, such as where a previous marriage was not properly dissolved and the applicant for the spousal benefit did not know that a prior marriage was not properly dissolved. When there is entitlement under this deemed valid marriage provision, the parties must be living in the same household at the time an application for benefits is filed.

Because of the Supreme Court decisions in *United States v. Windsor* and *Obergefell v. Hodges*, same-sex marriages are permitted and recognized in all states and U.S. territories, and the SSA is no longer prohibited from recognizing same-sex marriages for the purpose of determining entitlement to or eligibility for benefits. The internal rules of the SSA, the Program Operations Manual System (POMS), contain detailed instructions for agency staff on how to process claims that involve a same-sex marriage. In some cases, the SSA will consider a non-marital legal relationship, such as a civil union or domestic partnership, to be a marital relationship for benefit purposes. The complexity of these rules is beyond the scope of this section, and interested readers are urged to consult the POMS at § GN 00210.000, *et seq.*, located at https://secure.ssa.gov/poms.nsf/lnx/0200210000.

The spousal benefit is paid at the rate of 50% of the PIA of the insured worker, regardless of when the insured worker claimed his or her benefit. Thus, even if the insured worker claims his or her benefit at age 62, such that it is reduced by close to 25%, if the worker's spouse waits until his or her own FRA to claim the spousal benefit, the spousal benefit will be paid at the full 50% of the insured worker's PIA. However, the spousal benefit can be reduced if claimed prior to FRA or if the spouse is working, has not yet reached FRA, and exceeds the applicable annual threshold below which earned income is not counted.

## Ex-Spouses

A divorced spouse may also be eligible to receive a spousal benefit, but only if the marriage with the insured lasted for at least ten years prior to the finalization of divorce. The ex-spouse on whose account the benefit is claimed must either have filed for benefits or be at least age 62 and divorced for two years. The applicant for a spousal benefit in this situation cannot be married, unless he or she married another person who is entitled to a widow(er)'s, mother's, father's, children's disability, divorced spouse's, or parent's benefits.

If the divorced spouse remarried and that marriage terminated, through either divorce or death, the divorced spouse can be entitled or re-entitled to a spousal benefit, provided all of the other requirements for entitlement are met.

The benefit paid to an ex-spouse is paid at the same rate as a benefit paid to a married spouse: 50% of the PIA of the insured worker, subject to the same reductions that are applicable to benefits paid to a married spouse.

## Widow(er)s and Surviving Divorced Spouses

Widow(er)s are entitled to a survivor's benefit on the account of a deceased spouse if one of the following conditions are met:

- The widow(er) was married to the insured for at least nine months prior to the day of the insured's death unless the insured was expected to live for nine months and the death was accidental or in the line of duty or the insured and spouse were previously married for at least nine months or the insured and spouse would have been married but for the fact that the worker was unable to divorce a prior spouse who was in a mental institution (there are additional qualifications regarding this last condition),

- The widow(er) is the mother or father of the insured's child,
- The widow(er) legally adopted the insured's child who was under age 18 at the time, or,
- together with the insured, adopted a child who was then under age 18.

The widow(er)'s benefit is first available to a surviving spouse if the spouse is at least age 60, but *only if the widow(er) did not remarry prior to age 60!* (Remarriage at or after age 60 will *not* jeopardize entitlement to a widow(er)'s benefit.) If the widow(er) is disabled—that is, is unable to engage in any substantial gainful activity by reason of a mental or physical disease or defect that has lasted or is expected to last for at least 12 months—the widow(er)'s benefit is payable as early as age 50.

If claimed at or after FRA, the widow(er)'s benefit will, in most cases, be equal to the benefit amount received by the insured in the month prior to his or her death, increased only by a COLA if the increase was scheduled for the month of the insured's death. Thus, the widow(er)'s benefit reflects any increase in benefit that accrued to the insured due to the insured's delay in claiming a retirement benefit past FRA. Conversely, the widow(er)'s benefit will also reflect any reduction imposed on the benefit received by the insured prior to his death as a result of claiming the benefit prior to FRA. However, the reduction on this basis is limited to no more than 17.5% of the PIA of the deceased wage earner.

The widow(er)'s benefit is also available to a surviving divorced spouse who was married to the insured for at least ten years prior to the divorce.

## Child's Insurance Benefits

A minor or disabled child of an insured worker is entitled to receive a child's insurance benefit (CIB) if the insured is entitled to a retirement or disability benefit under the Social Security Act or has died. To be eligible, a child must be unmarried and under the age of 18, or under 19 and a full-time student in high school. A child who has a disability that began before age 22 (a "disabled adult child" or DAC) is also entitled to a special type of CIB, termed a "child's disability benefit" or CDB. The CDB need not begin prior to age 22. It is first payable to a child of any age (age 18 or older) so long as it can be established that the child was disabled prior to age 22 and that the disability has been continuous since that time. Even if it seems that continuous disability is not present in a given case because the child was employed for periods of time, it may still be available depending upon the circumstances.

For purposes of qualifying for this benefit, a child may be natural born, adopted, a stepchild, a grandchild, or a step-grandchild.

The benefit amount depends on whether the insured is alive or dead. If the insured is alive, the child will receive 50% of the insured's PIA. If the insured has died, the benefit amount is 75% of the deceased worker's PIA.

## Mother's, Father's, and Young Spouse's Benefits

If a CIB is paid to a minor child under the age of 16, or to a disabled child who is age 16 or above, the spouse of the wage earner on whose account the CIB is paid may be eligible to receive a benefit on that same earnings record. If the wage earner has died, the benefit payable is a "mother's or "father's" benefit and is paid to widow(er)s under FRA without any reduction for claiming prior to FRA. When the benefit is paid on the account of a living wage earner, the benefit amount is 50% of the wage earner's PIA; if the wage earner has died, the amount paid is 75% of the decedent's PIA.

## Parent's Benefits

A little-known benefit is that which is paid to the surviving parents of a deceased wage earner, if the parents were living with and dependent on the deceased prior to his or her death. The amount paid is 82.5% of the deceased wage earner's PIA, or 75% if a benefit is paid to both parents.

# Factors That Can Decrease or Increase Benefit Amounts

A number of factors can serve to increase or reduce the benefit that you can expect to receive from the SSA. Future benefits can be *increased* due to application of a COLA, a delay in the start of the benefit past FRA, and continuing to work at high earnings levels. However, future benefits can be reduced if claimed early; if received simultaneously with a pension based on earnings not covered by the Social Security Act, such as a school teacher or police officer pension; or if one continues to work while receiving a benefit prior to FRA. Benefits to auxiliaries can be reduced if the total amount of benefits paid to household members exceeds the maximum family benefit allowed for that year.

## Actuarial Reduction

The example highlighted in a previous section merely demonstrated how a PIA is calculated. But the PIA is not necessarily the benefit amount. The PIA *can* function as the benefit if the benefit is first paid at one's FRA—age 66 if you were born after January 1, 1943 and on or before January 2, 1955. However, more often than not, the PIA is only the starting point for determining the actual benefit amount. If benefits are claimed early, i.e., before FRA is attained, a percentage will be subtracted from the PIA to yield a lower benefit amount. This is referred to as "actuarial reduction." The amount of the reduction depends on the type of benefit being claimed and how many months prior to FRA the benefit is being claimed, i.e., the "reduction period." The longer the reduction period, the greater will be the permanent reduction of the benefit being claimed. Actuarial reduction impacts old-age benefits, spousal benefits, and widow(er)'s benefits.

An old-age benefit is reduced by 5/9 of 1% for each month up to the first 36 months of early claiming, and an additional 5/12 of 1% for each month thereafter. If your full retirement age is 66, the maximum reduction will be 25% of the PIA if you have a full 48-month reduction period. As explained earlier, most people claiming at age 62 will only have a 47-month reduction period because one must be at age 62 throughout a month in order to receive a benefit for that month. And, because one reaches a given age on the day before the anniversary of birth, only individuals born on the second day of the month can potentially have a full 48-month reduction period.

A spousal benefit (as well as a divorced spouse's benefit) is reduced by 25/36 of 1% for each month up to the first 36 months of early claiming, and an additional 5/12 of 1% for each month thereafter. If your FRA is 66, the maximum reduction will be 30% of the unreduced spousal benefit if you have a full 48-month reduction period.

> *Example*: Assume Jake and Jennifer are married. Jake reaches age 66 in July 2019, while Jennifer reaches age 66 in October 2022. Jake files a claim for RIB to begin in July 2019. His PIA is $2,400, and thus his benefit will also be $2,400. This is because the benefit is neither reduced for early claiming nor increased for delayed claiming. Jennifer can file a claim for a spousal benefit on Jake's account to begin in the same month. A spousal benefit is 50% the PIA of the wage earner—Jake, in this case. However, in Jennifer's case, it will be further reduced due to early claiming. Jennifer's reduction period is

43 months—the period from July 2019 up to February 2023, the month in which Jennifer reaches FRA. Note that because Jennifer was born in October 1956, her FRA is 66 years and 4 months. Thus, she reaches her FRA in February 2023. The reduction formula will look like this: $(36 \times (25/36) \times 1\%) + (7 \times (5/12) \times 1\%) = 27\ 11/12\%$. So, the spousal benefit of 50% of the PIA is further reduced by 27 11/12% = ½ × $2,400 − (.279166667 × ½ × $2,400) = $1,200 − $334.99 = $865.01. The result is rounded down to the nearest whole dollar for payment.

Note that even if Jake had claimed his own benefit at age 62, or alternatively, delayed his claim to later than age 66, it would not impact the amount of the spousal benefit payable to Jennifer. If he claimed at age 62, but Jennifer still waited until July 2019 to claim, the reduction of her benefit would still be 27 11/12%. Conversely, if Jake waited until age 70 to claim, Jennifer's spousal benefit would not be reduced at all! This is *not* because a delay in a claim by the primary wage earner directly results in a benefit increase to his or her spouse. Rather, it is because Jennifer cannot claim a spousal benefit until Jake files, and, because Jennifer will have reached her own FRA by the time Jake reaches age 70, the spousal benefit will no longer be reduced for early claiming.

Although the gradual increase in FRA will result in a gradual increase in the maximum amount by which an old-age or spousal benefit may be reduced (increasing from 25% to 30% for old-age benefits, and from 30% to 35% for spousal benefits), the same does not occur with respect to widow(er)'s benefits.

A widow(er)'s benefit (or a surviving divorced spouse's benefit) can be claimed as early as age 60 (or as early as age 50 if the widow(er) is disabled). The maximum reduction for a widow(er)'s benefit is 28.5% for a widow(er) claiming at age 60 (or for a disabled widow(er) claiming prior to age 60). As FRA increases, the maximum reduction remains at age 60; however, the monthly reduction amount is proportionately decreased. Thus, a widow(er)'s benefit for widow(er)s for whom FRA is age 66, will be subject to a monthly reduction factor of 57/14400, while the monthly reduction factor for someone whose FRA is at age 67 is 57/16800. Also note that the schedule that increases FRA for widow(er)s is two years behind the schedule in place for old-age benefits. The chart below shows the monthly reduction factor for widow(er)s and surviving divorced spouses, depending upon a widow(er)'s date of birth:

**Reduction Table for Widow(er)s and Surviving Divorced Spouses**

| Date of Birth | Full Benefit at Age | Maximum Reduction Period | Monthly Reduction Factor |
|---|---|---|---|
| 1/1/1940 or earlier | 65 | 60 months | $57/12000$ |
| 1/2/1940–1/1/1941 | 65 + 2 months | 62 months | $57/12400$ |
| 1/2/1941–1/1/1942 | 65 + 4 months | 64 months | $57/12800$ |
| 1/2/1942–1/1/1943 | 65 + 6 months | 66 months | $57/13200$ |
| 1/2/1943–1/1/1944 | 65 + 8 months | 68 months | $57/13600$ |
| 1/2/1944–1/1/1945 | 65 + 10 months | 70 months | $57/14000$ |
| 1/2/1945–1/1/1957 | 66 | 72 months | $57/14400$ |
| 1/2/1957–1/1/1958 | 66 + 2 months | 74 months | $57/14800$ |
| 1/2/1958–1/1/1959 | 66 + 4 months | 76 months | $57/15200$ |
| 1/2/1959–1/1/1960 | 66 + 6 months | 78 months | $57/15600$ |
| 1/2/1960–1/1/1961 | 66 + 8 months | 80 months | $57/16400$ |
| 1/2/1961–1/1/1962 | 66 + 10 months | 82 months | $57/16400$ |
| 1/2/1962 or later | 67 | 84 months | $57/16800$ |

# Maximum Family Benefits

The Social Security Act imposes a limitation on the amount of benefits that may be paid to members of a household, such that benefits paid to "auxiliaries" (dependents and survivors) may be reduced if the total amount of benefits exceeds a maximum benefit that is derived from the PIA of the wage earner. A wage earner's benefit is never reduced on account of the family maximum. The maximum family benefit (MFB) is determined by subjecting the wage earner's PIA to a benefit formula in the same way that AIME are converted into a PIA. The MFB formula, however, is more complex, with three bend points. For most individuals reading this book, the MFB will work out to be approximately 175% to 180% of one's current PIA. In general, the MFB is calculated by applying the bend points for the year in which the insured worker reaches age 62. The PIA, prior to any COLAs, is then inserted into the MFB formula, and the result is then increased by any COLAs applied after the worker reached age 62. After the MFB is determined, the wage earner's PIA (after application of COLAs) is subtracted from the MFB, and the remainder is available to be divided among auxiliary beneficiaries. Note that the MFB in disability cases uses a less generous formula: it is 150% of the wage earner's PIA.

> *Example*: Donald and Melanie have four children. Melanie does not work outside of the home, and two of their children are over age 18. Donald has a PIA of $2,600 before any COLAs and files a claim for retirement benefits at age 68 in July 2019, when Melanie is at age 57, one child is at age 14, and another child is at age 17. What is the benefit amount that each will receive?
>
> Donald will receive a benefit that reflects COLAs from 2013, the year in which he reached age 62, and is further increased by 24 delayed retirement credits (DRCs) due to waiting 24 months past the month in which he reached his FRA before claiming retirement benefits. Because each DRC is worth 2/3 of 1%, his benefit is increased by 16%. Donald's PIA of $2,600 is increased by COLAs of 1.5%, 1.7%, 0%, 0.3%, 2.0% and 2.8% since 2013 to result in a cost-of-living-increased PIA of $2,822.62. That amount is then increased by 16% to $3,274.24 on account of delayed claiming. This amount is then rounded down by statute to $3,274.00 for the benefit amount.

The MFB is calculated by inserting the PIA of $2,600 in the 2013 MFB formula to yield $4,549.77. Note that this is very close to 175% of the PIA, which is $4,550. The MFB, as determined by the 2013 MFB formula, is then increased by cost-of-living increases since 2013 to yield the actual MFB of $4,939.10. So, to determine the amount available for other family members, the PIA (as increased by COLAs) is subtracted from the MFB (as increased by COLAs and rounded down to the nearest $0.10, as required by statute): $4,549.70 – $2,822.62 = $2,116.58, which is rounded down to $2,116.50. (Note that it is the *PIA* that is subtracted from the MFB to yield what is available to pay auxiliaries and *not* the actual benefit paid to the wage earner!)

Three family members are entitled to a benefit on Donald's account: the two minor children and Melanie. (Melanie is entitled to an unreduced spouse's benefit, despite not having reached age 62, because she has in her care at least one child under age 16.) Each of these benefits is ordinarily 50% of the wage earner's PIA. However, because the PIA is $2,822.62, three times one half of that, $4,233.93, is well above the $2,116.50 that is available for auxiliary beneficiaries under the MFB rule; thus, each auxiliary will receive a benefit that is 1/3 of $2,116.50 (the remainder after subtracting the PIA from the MFB), which is $705, after rounding down to the nearest whole dollar as required by law.

Thus, the total benefit paid to this family will be Donald's benefit of $3,274 plus $2,115 paid to family members. Although the total of $5,389 exceeds the MFB of $4,549.70, as calculated above, this result reflects that the MFB is not the actual maximum available to an entire family but is a statutorily derived amount, based on the PIA, from which the PIA is subtracted in order to determine the remainder available to auxiliaries.

The SSA provides a detailed explanation of the MFB formula here: https://www.ssa.gov/OACT/COLA/familymax.html, with a link to a table that displays bend points for prior years.

In cases where both parents have claimed a benefit, the family maximum benefits on *both* accounts are combined to yield a combined maximum family benefit. This combined maximum can be helpful to reduce the limitation imposed by the MFB in cases where there are multiple children eligible for benefits.

In addition to the wage earner, benefits paid to certain beneficiaries are not reduced on account of the MFB (nor are benefits to other auxiliaries reduced on account of such payments): a divorced spouse, a surviving divorced spouse, and a legal spouse when a deemed spouse is entitled.

## Pensions Based on Non-Covered Earnings (WEP and GPO)

Your benefit can be reduced if you also receive a pension that is based on earnings that were not subject to Social Security tax. These earnings—termed "non-covered earnings"—could be from a state or local government employer, including many school districts, which chose not to opt in to the Social Security program. These pensions can serve to reduce your own benefit under the Windfall Elimination Provision (WEP) and can also serve to reduce a benefit you receive as a spouse or widow(er) under the Government Pension Offset (GPO) provision. A pension received from a foreign employer is also subject to the WEP but not to the GPO.

The rationale for these reductions is that the Social Security benefit formula is a progressive formula, which replaces a higher proportion of pre-retirement earnings for individuals with lower lifetime earnings. (Although higher earnings up to an annual threshold will always yield a higher benefit.) However, if the reason one has lower lifetime earnings is not due to toiling in a low-paying job for many years, but rather, is due to not having worked for a number of years in covered employment, the benefit amount does not reflect a lifetime of low wages. A person with really high lifetime wages may only be entitled to a Social Security benefit of $1,600, rather than $3,200, if he spent 20 years in local government employment that was not part of the Social Security program. However, that worker will also likely receive a pension from non-covered employment that could amount to as much as $3,000 to $6,000 per month. The wage earner who flipped burgers in a fast-food restaurant for 35 years, however, will receive no pension and is likely to have meager savings. Replacing a higher proportion of his or her pre-retirement earnings is far more critical than it is to the wage earner who also receives a pension based on non-covered employment.

The reduction under the GPO is ⅔ of the amount of the pension. However, the WEP reduction is far more complex. In most cases, the reduction under the WEP is the lesser of one-half the amount of the pension or one-half of the first bend point in the Social Security benefit formula for the year in which the wage earner reached age 62, increased only by COLAs since that time. Wage earners with at least 30 years of "substantial earnings," are exempt from operation of the WEP (but not from the GPO). Wage earners with substantial earnings for at least 21 to 29 years will have a gradually reduced reduction under the WEP. "Substantial earnings" has a very specific meaning under the Social Security Act and is based on yet another complex formula.

Note that any reduction under the WEP or the GPO is only experienced as a result of the beneficiary's receipt of a pension that is based on his or her *own* non-covered earnings—not those of a spouse.

*Example 1*: Abe dies in the month in which he reaches age 70 after a long career as a high school physics teacher. His surviving spouse, Sara, is an attorney who has always been in private practice. Abe received a public teacher's pension of

$5,000 per month. This is a pension based on non-covered earnings. Abe also received a Social Security benefit based on his earnings as an education consultant and part-time instructor at a private university, which he first claimed at age 66, his FRA. Abe's PIA of $2,000 was reduced under the WEP on account of his receipt of a pension based on non-covered earnings. The reduction was 1/2 of the first bend point in the Social Security benefit formula for the year in which Abe reached age 62—2010. In that year, the first bend point was $761. Abe's benefit in 2019 would have been $2,287.66, had there been no reduction on account of his receiving a pension based on non-covered earnings. This amount reflects COLA increases since 2010. This amount, however, is reduced to $1,852.43 on account of the WEP. When Abe dies at age 70, Sara will be eligible to receive a Social Security widow's benefit on Abe's account. The amount that Sara will receive is the full amount of Abe's PIA, prior to any reduction under the WEP. This is because a pension based on non-covered earnings is no longer being paid to Abe. Thus, Sara's widow's benefit will be $2,287 after rounding down to the nearest whole dollar. Note that Sara's widow's benefit is *not* reduced under the GPO. This is because Sara is not receiving a pension based on her own non-covered work. Even if Abe's pension plan pays a widow's benefit to Sara, Sara's widow's benefit under the Social Security Act will not be reduced. That is because the GPO is triggered only when a pension is paid based on the beneficiary's *own* non-covered employment.

*Example 2*: Assume the same facts as in Example 1. However, also assume that Sara receives a pension based on her own non-covered earnings. That pension is $4,500 per month. Given this pension amount, will Sara be able to collect a widow's benefit on Abe's account? The answer is "No." The widow's benefit is $2,287. However, under the GPO, that benefit is reduced by ⅔ of the pension amount. Two-thirds of the pension amount is $3,000, which is greater than the widow's benefit. Thus, no widow's benefit can be paid in this case.

Further details on the WEP, including a list of what amounts to substantial earnings for each year, can be found in the following government publication: https://www.ssa.gov/pubs/EN-05-10045.pdf. Additional details about the GPO may be found here: https://www.ssa.gov/pubs/EN-05-10007.pdf.

If you know that you are going to receive a pension based on non-covered earnings, you will need to notify the SSA. If you don't, it will eventually find out about the pension through computer matching programs, and you could be liable for a very large overpayment that you first learn about many years, even decades, after you first become entitled to benefits. Notifying the SSA that you expect to receive such a pension at some point in the future is not sufficient. You must notify Social Security when you actually apply for and begin to receive the pension. This is best done using Form SSA-150 (https://www.ssa.gov/forms/ssa-150.pdf). If you receive a foreign pension, you should file Form SSA-308 (https://www.ssa.gov/forms/ssa-308.pdf). In the event the GPO is triggered, you should also file Form SSA-3885 (https://www.ssa.gov/forms/ssa-3885.pdf). When filing these forms (or any other form) with the SSA, make a copy, hand-deliver both to a local field office, make sure both copies are time and date stamped, and keep one copy for yourself. The agency may fail to record the form and then, years later, discover that you have a pension and assess an overpayment. Proof of notifications demonstrates that you were not at fault with respect to the overpayment, which is the first step in determining if an overpaid person is entitled to a waiver of the overpayment in the event the individual cannot afford to repay the overpayment.

Unless you qualify for one of the exceptions, you should expect to see your benefits decrease following your notice to the SSA that you are about to receive a pension based on non-covered earnings. If that doesn't happen, be sure to save a portion of your benefits for repayment to the government because you will inevitably receive an overpayment notice.

## Working While Receiving Retirement Benefits

So, as you approach your 62nd birthday, you may be thinking that an extra $2,000 to $3,000 a month in retirement benefits looks very attractive, even if you have to take a cut because you are claiming the benefit prior to FRA. You are thinking that even if you don't need the money now, you can invest the funds and obtain a higher "return" than what you would receive in delayed retirement credits by delaying your claim. While it is dubious that you would get a higher "return" by investing your benefits rather than delaying a claim (more on this point in a later section), there is another, more serious issue: the extent to which you can receive a Social Security retirement benefit while continuing to work.

Social Security "old-age" (retirement benefits on your own account) and spousal benefits can be claimed as early as age 62; widow(er)'s benefits may be claimed even earlier, at age 60. However, if you receive any of these benefits prior to FRA, your benefit is subject to reduction if you continue to work and have earnings above certain thresholds. There are two earnings tests: one for years prior to the year in which one reaches FRA and one for the year in which FRA is attained. There are also additional rules for beneficiaries who are self-employed.

In general, the income that counts as earnings for purposes of the earnings test are (a) gross wages for services rendered in a taxable year and (b) all net earnings from self-employment for that taxable year minus any net loss from self-employment for the same year.

# Wage Income

The general rule is that for beneficiaries who have not yet reached the year in which FRA is attained, earnings above an annual threshold will result in a reduction of benefits by $1 for every $2 of earnings over the threshold. For beneficiaries in the year that FRA is attained, the reduction in benefits is $1 for every $3 of earnings above a higher threshold, but *only with respect to earnings prior to the month in which FRA is attained.*

In 2018, the lower threshold, applicable to workers who have not yet reached the year in which they will attain FRA, was $17,040. This threshold has increased in 2019 to $17,640. The higher threshold, applicable to workers who are reaching FRA in a given year, was $45,360 in 2018 and has increased to $46,920 for 2019.

> *Example 1*: Harry decides to retire and collect Social Security retirement benefits when he reaches age 65 in July 2018, but he continues to work part-time, earning $2,500 a month. If Harry's PIA is $2,600, what will his monthly benefit be in 2018 and in 2019? The answer is derived by first calculating the benefit amount that reflects a reduction for early claiming. Because Harry is claiming his benefit exactly one year prior to his FRA, the reduction is $(5/9) \times (1/100) \times 12 \times \$2,600 = \$173.33$. This amount is subtracted from the PIA to yield the monthly benefit amount of $2,426.67. This amount is then subject to reduction because Harry's earnings exceed the threshold of allowable earnings not subject to reduction. In 2018, the reduction was $1 for every $2 of earnings over the lower threshold. And, because this is the initial year for which benefits are paid to Harry, he is subject to a monthly earnings test, of $17,040 + 12, which is $1,420. Harry's monthly earnings of $2,500 exceed this lower threshold by $1,080 ($2,500 − $1,420 = $1,080). Because benefits are reduced by $1 for every $2 of earnings that exceed the threshold, the actual benefit that is payable is $2,426.67 − $(0.5 \times \$1,080) = \$1,886.67$, which is then rounded down to the nearest whole dollar.
>
> For 2019, Harry's actuarially reduced benefit of $2,426.67 is first increased by the annual COLA of 2.8% to $2,494.62 $(1.028 \times \$2,426.67 = \$2,494.62)$. The applicable annual exempt amount is $46,920. Harry's total earnings prior

to the month in which FRA is attained (July) are six times his monthly earnings of $2,500, which is $15,000. Because $15,000 is less than the annual threshold, there is no reduction of Harry's benefit on account of having earnings in excess of the applicable threshold.

Thresholds for the coming year are announced by the SSA in mid-October and published in the Federal Register by the end of the month. These amounts may be found at this website, along with other annual determinations: https://www.ssa.gov/oact/cola /autoAdj.html.

To obtain the reduction amount, earnings above the applicable threshold are divided by two for years prior to the year FRA is attained and are divided by three for the year in which FRA is attained. Any fractional portion is rounded down to the nearest whole dollar.

The rules governing what counts and what does not count as income for the purpose of the earnings test are too complex to fully cover in this section. Some of the more common issues will be addressed below. However, for details, the interested reader should consult internal agency rules—the POMS— at § RS 02500.000, *et seq*. The table of contents for this section is located here: https://secure.ssa.gov/apps10/poms.nsf /subchapterlist!openview&restricttocategory=03025.

Generally, all wage income is counted, unless it is specifically excluded. Wages are counted in the taxable year for which they are earned and not for the year in which they are paid. Thus, if you retire beginning on January 1, 2019, but receive a paycheck in January for work performed in the prior month, December 2018, the earnings will not count for 2019.

Dismissal, severance, or termination pay all count as wages, as does back pay (including back pay under a statute, such as the Americans with Disabilities Act and the Age Discrimination in Employment Act). However, back pay is counted for the period in which it *should* have been paid. Worker's Compensation payments are *not* wages. Sick and disability payments *do* count as wages for the first six calendar months after the last calendar month in which the employee worked for that employer, but not thereafter.

Workers retiring prior to the end of the year, who have pre-retirement earnings that exceed the annual threshold may still receive a benefit if their monthly earnings following retirement are less than 1/12 of the applicable annual threshold. This "monthly earnings test" allows payment of benefits to a beneficiary if he or she has considerable earnings prior to the month of entitlement, but monthly earnings that are less than 1/12 of the applicable exempt amount once retirement begins. Any month in which earnings are less than 1/12 of the applicable exempt amount is called a "non-service month." The monthly earnings test applies if the beneficiary has one or more non-service months in a "grace year." A grace year can be an initial grace year, a grace year following a break in entitlement, or a termination grace year. Most beneficiaries will have only an initial grace year, which is the first taxable year in which a beneficiary is entitled to a benefit prior to FRA, has a month of entitlement in which the beneficiary has no wages in excess of the monthly exempt amount, and does not perform "substantial services in self-employment," which is discussed in the next section.

# Self-Employment Income

The annual earnings tests that apply for wage income, described above, also apply for self-employment income. However, the treatment of self-employment income is subject to a number of additional rules.

Self-employment earnings are counted the same way for earnings test purposes as they are for tax purposes. Thus, business income that is excluded when computing net earnings from self-employment (NESE) is also excluded for earnings test purposes. NESE are ordinarily counted for earnings test purposes in the taxable year the earnings are received. However, self-employment income that is received after the initial year of entitlement to retirement benefits can be excluded for deduction purposes from gross earnings in the taxable year received if the income is not attributable to services performed after the initial month of entitlement.

As explained above, the monthly earnings test is generally applicable in the initial year of retirement. However, if a self-employed individual engages in "substantial services" once benefits begin, benefits can be suspended even if no NESE accrues from the work performed.

A retired person performs substantial services in a month in which he or she devotes (a) more than 45 hours to the business or (b) from 15 through 45 hours to a business in a "highly skilled occupation." If services are less than 15 hours per month, they are deemed to not be substantial. Services greater than 45 hours may not necessarily be substantial if the person's monthly earnings are readily determinable and if the earnings, figured on a time basis, are equal to or less than the monthly exempt amount. However, for most self-employed people, monthly earnings are not readily determinable, and thus this exception does not apply in most cases.

How the earnings test works can best be understood by working through a few examples:

> *Example 1*: Let's assume you reach FRA in October 2022 and decided to file a claim for RIB on your own earnings record at age 62 in June 2018. Let's further assume that you will have wage income of $90,000 in 2019, that you plan to continue working, and that you have a PIA of $2,600. How does the earnings test impact the benefit you can expect to receive?
>
> First, your benefit would *not* be $2,600. Your calculated PIA at age 62, $2,600, is the *unreduced* benefit amount that you could expect to receive at your FRA (plus increases due to any COLAs between age 62 and your FRA). Your expected benefit at age 62 will be reduced under the benefit formula discussed above to reflect a 51-month reduction period (assuming you are born on a day that is not the second day

of the month). The reduction period is not 52 months because, as discussed above, you must be at age 62 throughout the entire month in order to receive a benefit for that month. The reduction formula is $((5/9) \times 1\% \times 36) + ((5/12) \times 1\% \times 15) \times \$2,600 = (20\% + 6.25\%) \times \$2,600 = \$682.50$. This amount is subtracted from your PIA of \$2,600 to yield a benefit of \$1,917.50, which is then rounded down to \$1,917.

If you have earnings of \$90,000 in 2018, and if you continue to work after your first month of entitlement, which would be July 2018, your benefit would be subject to reduction by \$1 for every \$2 of earnings over the 2019 threshold of \$17,640. The amount over the threshold is \$72,360 (\$90,000 – \$17,640). That amount is then divided by 2 to yield the reduction amount of \$36,180. With benefits of \$1,917 for six months in 2018, the total 2018 benefit, \$11,502 (6 × \$1,917), would be reduced to zero by a reduction amount of \$36,180.

In this example, it is clear that you would not be able to receive a benefit in 2019 if you filed a claim for benefits but continued to work. However, you might think that it would still be worthwhile to claim a benefit so that your spouse could receive a spousal benefit. However, when a worker's benefits are reduced under the earnings test, so too are auxiliary benefits. That is, the excess is charged to the total family benefit. Thus, the spousal benefit of \$1,300 (remember, the spousal benefit is 50% of the PIA and *not* 50% of the actual benefit paid to the primary wage earner) over a six-month period, which amounts to \$7,800, would also be reduced to zero because the total family benefit of \$19,302 (\$11,502 + \$7,800) would be reduced to zero by the \$36,180 reduction amount. In practice, benefit reductions due to the earnings test are first applied to auxiliary benefits before they are applied to the worker's benefit.

*Example 2*: Assume the same facts as in Example 1, except that you actually stop working in the first month of entitlement,

July 2018, but return to work in October and November to work on a special project for which you are paid a salary of $5,000 per month. In this case, 2018 would be an initial grace year because you have a non-service month following your entitlement to retirement benefits. In this case, the monthly retirement test would apply for the months of October and November. The monthly threshold is $17,040 divided by 12, which is $1,420. Your monthly earnings of $5,000 would exceed the threshold by $3,580. The reduction amount would be $1,790. Thus, you could expect to have your benefit of $1,917 reduced by $1,790 to $127. This assumes that only you are collecting a benefit. If your spouse claims a spousal benefit on your account, her unreduced benefit would be $1,300 prior to any reduction due to *her* early claiming. Let's assume for this example that she is already at her own FRA, so the benefit will not be actuarially reduced. Her benefit of $1,300 will be reduced first, followed by a reduction of your benefit by the remaining reduction amount of $490 ($1,790 – $1,300).

Note that a dependent's benefit is also subject to reduction based on the dependent's own earnings. However, the benefit of the wage earner would not ever be reduced on account of the work activity of a dependent.

As a practical matter, if you expect to return to work, you will need to promptly notify the SSA and let it know what your earnings are each month. You must also inform the SSA as to when you will no longer be working so that it doesn't assume that you continue to work at the same earnings level in subsequent years.

# Taxation of Benefits

A Social Security benefit may be tax-free, or a portion of the benefit may be includable in gross income, depending on the amount of a beneficiary's "provisional income" for a taxable year. Provisional income is a beneficiary's "modified adjusted gross income," plus 50% of the beneficiary's Social Security benefit. Modified adjusted gross income is adjusted gross income plus tax-exempt interest, foreign earned income exclusion, adoption benefits, and U.S. possessions source income.

Social Security benefits are not subject to tax if a beneficiary's provisional income is $25,000 or less for single individuals, or $32,000 or less for married couples filing jointly. Fifty percent of Social Security benefits is includable in gross income for single individuals with provisional income greater than $25,000 but not more than $34,000, and for married couples with provisional income greater than $32,000 but not more than $44,000. Single individuals and married couples with income in excess of $34,000 and $44,000, respectively, will need to include 85% of their Social Security benefits in gross income.

U.S. citizens who are residents of the following countries are exempt from U.S. tax on their benefits: Canada, Egypt, Germany, Ireland, Israel, Italy (but only if the taxpaper is also a citizen of Italy), Romania, and the United Kingdom.

# Disability Benefits

Insured workers who are disabled are eligible to receive a disability benefit at any age prior to FRA. And, if one is insured and disabled under the Social Security Act—that is, unable to engage in any *substantial gainful activity* by reason of any medically determinable physical or mental impairment that can be expected to result in death or that has lasted or can be expected to last for a continuous period of not less than 12 months—it may be more advantageous for the retiree at age 62 to claim the disability benefit rather than a retirement benefit. That is because a retirement benefit prior to one's FRA, which is currently age 66, but is gradually increasing to age 67 beginning with those born after January 1, 1955, will be reduced for early claiming, while the disability benefit will be the larger PIA.

# Deeming and Benefit Claiming Strategies

When considering the filing of a claim for retirement benefits, it is important to consider what other benefits might be triggered when a claim is filed. "Other benefits" can refer to others who might be eligible on your account as well as other benefits to which you might become entitled.

Your claim for retirement benefits might result in a spouse becoming eligible for a benefit on your account, assuming the spouse is at age 62. If you have minor or disabled adult children, they, too, would become eligible to receive a benefit on your account once you file a claim for benefits. Conversely, if you file a claim for a retirement benefit, you may also be deemed to be filing a claim for a spousal benefit and vice versa under the "deeming rule." Generally, under this rule, a claim for a retirement benefit is deemed to also be a claim for a spousal benefit, and a claim for a spousal benefit is deemed to also be a claim for a retirement benefit. The retirement benefit on one's own account is always paid first. However, if the spousal benefit is higher and, if the other spouse has already become entitled to his or her own retirement benefit, then you would be eligible to receive that portion of the spousal benefit that exceeds your own benefit, i.e., the "spousal excess."

The deeming rule is applicable, generally, to all individuals born *after* January 1, 1954. Individuals born on or before January 1, 1954, are subject to the rule only if a claim for benefits is filed prior to FRA. At FRA, one is permitted to file what is called a "restricted application for spousal benefits only." The advantage of this strategy is that it permits the claimant to receive a benefit on his or her spouse's earnings record while allowing his or her own benefit to grow. Exercising this strategy has the potential to boost cumulative household benefits by as much as $50,000 to $60,000 in the present value of the cumulative household benefit over a couple's anticipated lifetimes. However, as will be discussed below, it is not always readily apparent that it will be advantageous to exercise this strategy. Much depends on the relative disparity between the earnings levels and ages of the spouses.

# When Should You File a Claim for Social Security Retirement Benefits?

All that you have read until this point regarding Social Security benefits explains how a benefit is calculated and what may serve to reduce or increase the benefit. But it does not explain to you *when* you should claim the benefit. The answer to that question depends on a number of factors: your income needs, your goals outside of work, your life expectancy, the benefit amount, your ability and desire to continue working, your income resources outside of Social Security, your personal risk tolerance and degree of investment savvy, the availability of other Social Security benefits, such as a widow's or disability benefit, your ability to boost a benefit by continuing to work, the age and earnings disparity between spouses, and the impact of a pension from non-covered work. There is no "one-size-fits-all" response. However, if your goal is to maximize the cumulative household benefit you can expect to receive over your anticipated lifetime and the lifetime of anyone else potentially eligible for a benefit on your account, there are some general principles to consider.

Social Security benefits have both an investment and an insurance component. The insurance component is to ensure that one does not run out of money with increased age. The investment component provides an inflation-protected, government-guaranteed benefit that increases gradually from age 62 to age 70. Starting at one's FRA, that growth is 8% per year.

Your decision when to claim may depend as much on your financial situation and health as it does on anything else. If you are in good health and financially secure, your concern will be less about income inadequacy and more about maximizing benefits and a break-even analysis (a determination as to the point at which cumulative benefits begin to exceed the amount that would have been received had the benefit been claimed at age 62). However, if you are struggling financially, the temptation will be great to collect early. Yet, the better strategy is to continue working, defer Social Security, and deplete assets if necessary. This is because each month of deferral is like buying an additional inflation-adjusted annuity. Delaying a claim also has a tax benefit in that a larger proportion of one's monthly income needs comes from Social Security, resulting in a larger proportion of those income needs being subject to the 50% or 85% inclusion for income tax purposes.

Before deciding on a claiming strategy, it will be helpful to know, at least, what you can expect to receive as a benefit. The SSA has made this easy in recent years by setting up an online portal through which any wage earner can check his or her earnings record for accuracy and learn the expected amount of the retirement benefit on his or her own account at key ages, such as age 62, FRA, and age 70. In order to set up an account, go to https://secure.ssa.gov/RIL/SiView.action and click on "Create an Account." Armed with the benefit information gleaned through this portal, you can now begin to consider when to file a claim for retirement benefits.

For a single individual, if the goal is to maximize cumulative household benefits, the answer as to when to file is clear: delay a claim until age 70 unless your health is so poor that you won't make it to the break-even point, which will be around age 81. However, for couples, the answer to the question "When should I file for Social Security?" is not so clear. This is especially true for households with two wage earners. If you consider that between ages 62 and 70 there are 96 months in which a retirement benefit can be claimed, and that either spouse could file a claim in any one of those months, there are a total of 9,120 permutations of claiming strategies. Even if you discount strategies that involve filing a claim prior to FRA, for a couple in which both spouses reach FRA at age 67, there are still 1,260 possible claiming strategies. And, each strategy will produce its own cumulative lifetime benefit and its own set of break-even points. (Where the claims of two individuals are considered, there is no one break-even point, because the break-even point for the cumulative household benefit depends upon when one's spouse dies. This makes sense: if a spouse dies young, the surviving spouse will have to live longer in order to break even in terms of the cumulative household benefit.)

Because of the large number of permutations of strategies, it is not usually possible to accurately guess which claiming strategy will be the most advantageous in terms of maximizing cumulative household benefits over the anticipated lifetimes of both spouses. As a result, a cottage industry in benefit maximization software has cropped up. Most of these programs are poorly designed and fail to account for all the factors that can serve to increase or reduce benefits. Although each and every one of these programs has some flaws, two programs have proven themselves to be more reliable than their competitors: Maximize My Social Security (https://maximizemy socialsecurity.com/) and Social Security Timing (https://www.covi sum.com/social-security-timing). These programs do have a learning curve and their own advantages and disadvantages: Maximize My Social Security assumes death always occurs in December of the year that is at the end of one's projected life expectancy and does not publish break-even points with its results, while Social Security Timing does not test for every single permutation, but rather, looks at birth month and first month of the year combinations. However, Social Security Timing provides month-by-month cash flow charts and a graphic that indicates which strategy (for up to four strategies) is most advantageous for a given death-age combination for both spouses. Maximize My Social Security uses annual cash flow charts. On the other hand, Maximize My Maximize My Social Security is the only commercially available program to provide a recommended strategy for families with minor or disabled adult children. However, that program does not yet account for benefits that the disabled child may already be receiving, such as Supplemental Security Income (SSI) benefits or Disability Insurance Benefits (DIB) under Title II of the Social Security Act. To be certain of the result in cases where benefits for minor or disabled adult children are not implicated, it is best to use both programs so that the results of one program can be used as a check against the other.

# Filing a Claim for Benefits

A claim for benefits may be filed online, by telephone, or in person. While filing online or by telephone is, obviously, more convenient, filing in person will enable you to make sure, on the spot, that the claim is accurate and is exactly the type of claim that you intend. This can be of particular concern if you are filing a restricted application for spousal benefits because there is no specific box on the application form for this option. It is something that has to be specified in the remarks section of the online form. In person, you can make sure that that specification is added to the paper receipt that you will be handed at the end of the interview. Another trap to be wary of is the boilerplate that appears on all forms that the applicant is filing for *all* benefits for which he or she is eligible. That won't be true in a case where a restricted application for spousal benefits only is being filed. When you file in person, you can make clear the *month* for which you wish benefits to begin. You may file a claim for benefits up to four months in advance, and you can also file retroactively for up to six months. However, you may not file retroactively for any month that precedes FRA.

One final point that all applicants should know is that if you have made a mistake or wish to change your mind, you have one year from your benefit entitlement date (the month for which benefits begin, which may be retroactive, and *not* necessarily the application date or the benefit award date!) within which to withdraw your claims for benefits. If a claim for benefits is withdrawn, all benefits received on that claim must be repaid.